The Golden Voices of Football

WWJ

Ted Patterson
Foreword by Keith Jackson

The Golden Voices of Football

Ted Patterson
Foreword by Keith Jackson

Publisher: **Peter L. Bannon**

Senior managing editor: **Susan M. Moyer**

Art director: **K. Jeffrey Higgerson**

Graphic designer: **Christine Mohrbacher**

Developmental editor: **Elisa Bock Laird**

Photo editor: **Erin Linden-Levy**

Imaging: **Kerri Baker and Christine Mohrbacher**

Cover design: **Kerri Baker**

Acquisitions editor: **Mike Pearson**

Marketing manager: **Scott Rauguth**

Front cover photo courtesy of WWJ Newsradio 950
Endsheets artwork courtesy of Robert T. Handville
ISBN: 1-58261-744-9

Dedicated in memory of my nephew, Bret Scanlon, who loved football and all sports and who left us suddenly and tragically on Easter Sunday 2002. He will be with us always.

Contents

Foreword

In the psyche of every male there hides the lust to be a "warrior" at least once in his life. Maybe not one who rides the high plains on the white horse slashing the impurities from the morning air with his own Excalibur—but one who seizes and exercises that moment that squares his shoulders and marks his entry to the rest of his life.

There is no greater moment for the warrior who chooses the gridiron on which to seek his chance to create fate…than emerging from the tunnel into the glittering sunlight to the thunderous roars from the faithful…prancing across the absorbing greensward… stalwart and undefeated…for no blow has been struck…yet!

To read this book compiled by Ted Patterson is to meet and understand the word mechanics who have at times become poets in creating their word pictures of a sports event and especially the game of football.

You also get to know the ones who invented that happy escape from proper grammar, which we call vernacular…heh heh!

Have fun remembering!

Keith Jackson, 2004

Keith Jackson hard at work in 1958 on a DC-7 headed for London.
Photo courtesy of Keith Jackson

Credits and Acknowledgments

Over three decades have gone by since the original inception of this book. There are many people who helped with this project then and many who have made important contributions some 35 years later. Certainly the announcers and radio-TV people who gave me both time and encouragement are at the top of the list. The late Harold Arlin, Tom Manning, France Laux, Lindsey Nelson, Harry Wismer, Ty Tyson, Marty Glickman, Mel Allen, Jack Buck, and Joe Tucker head the list. Curt Gowdy, Chuck Thompson, Keith Jackson, Gil Stratton, Ray Christensen, Merle Harmon, Ernie Harwell, and Bob Wolff are still active and very supportive. Keith Jackson went above and beyond by writing the foreword and introducing the audio CD. Keith retired once from the broadcast booth. Let's hope he never does it again.

Traveling around on a shoestring budget meant relying on college friends in many cities. The Zirpolis in New York, Gallos in Pittsburgh, and Browns near Cooperstown all provided wonderful accommodations.

A huge thank you goes to Mike Pearson and his colleagues at Sports Publishing, who believed that the golden voices should be preserved for posterity and have enthusiastically produced a quality tandem of baseball and football broadcasting histories. Special thanks to editor Elisa Bock Laird.

Making it all happen on the audio production side is producer John Vincent, who had to deal with recording methods from 35 years ago and back and somehow adapt them for today's compact disc technology. John deserves a great round of applause. So does Ken Needle, Will Fastie, and Michael Patterson, all of whom got me up to date with modern-day computer wizardry.

Helping me track down several of the audio highlights was longtime friend and fellow collector John Miley, who helped fill in several gaps in the assembly of the actual voice recordings. I've known John for almost 30 years, and it is great to finally work with him on this project.

Thanks also go out to several sports information departments at Michigan, West Virginia, Texas, Minnesota, Georgia, Notre Dame, and Iowa.

Thanks to Bill Little of the University of Texas sports information department; Bill Sansing, a key component of the old Humble Network in the Southwest; and Dale Miller of the West Virginia Mountaineer network. Thanks to Halsey Hall biographer Stew Thornley.

Last but not least, "Gal Friday" Kathy Fox, who helped with the original research gathering and utilized her great secretarial skills some 35 years ago, and who came back for more as she cruised the Internet searching for the never-to-be-forgotten sportscasting pioneers.

Introduction

Growing up in the 1950s in a football-crazy state like Ohio meant two things during the football season. One was listening to the Ohio State Buckeyes on Saturday afternoons, and the other was either watching or listening to the NFL Cleveland Browns on Sunday. Thanks to broadcasters such as Tom Manning, Bob Neal, Ken Coleman, and Gib Shanley, the exploits of Howard "Hopalong" Cassady, Otto Graham, and Jim Brown came alive on radio and television. For a youngster hooked on sports, whose only connection to pro and college football was the annual *Street and Smiths* magazine, *Sports Illustrated*, and *Sport Magazine* as well as the yearly diet of Bowman and Topps football cards, radio quickly became the favorite connection to the sport of football. Broadcasters such as Bill Stern and Harry Wismer did the big national games involving Notre Dame, Army-Navy, Ohio State-Michigan, as well as the bowl lineup.

By the mid- to late 1950s, big-game rivalries were being telecast on Saturday afternoons with Lindsey Nelson and Red Grange at the microphones. One of my great memories was watching Lindsey and Red describe Dick Lynch running around the right side and giving Notre Dame a 7-0 win over Oklahoma that snapped the Sooners' 47 straight win streak in 1957. This was long before the days of isolated cameras, stop action and slow motion reruns, end zone cameras, and blimp shots. It was just a couple of cameras and the announcers.

During the week, the only televised football shows were a prognostication show hosted by former Notre Dame coach Frank Leahy, in which his little cartoon pal, "Fumbles," would announce who would win the game and by how many touchdowns. Legendary Browns quarterback Otto Graham hosted a weekly show with his wife, Pamela, called, *At Home with the Grahams*, which didn't hit the Xs and Os in very much depth. That was left to Ken Coleman, who hosted the weekly *Quarterback Club*, which reviewed the past week's Browns game and

Broadcasters Red Grange and Lindsey Nelson cover the 1954 Cotton Bowl where Rice played Alabama. *Photo courtesy of the University of Tennessee Sports Information Department*

Frank Leahy (above) hosted a television show that predicted who would win the upcoming weekend games. Ken Coleman (below) hosted a show called *Quarterback Club* that analyzed and previewed the play of the Cleveland Browns. *Background photo courtesy of the University of Notre Dame; foreground photo courtesy of the author's collection*

previewed the next with a couple of players as guests. Today's fans, brought up on *SportsCenter* and wall-to-wall game broadcasts, would have been stunned at the paucity of football coverage. Baseball was the national pastime, and football took a backseat.

Coupled with the rise of the NFL was the impact on the sport by NFL Films. It was in its infancy stage in the late 1950s, comprised of a 30-minute highlight show late on Sunday mornings, recapping the games from the Sunday before. Jim Leaming was the announcer, and I marveled at his colorful descriptions. "Johnny Sample purloined the pigskin and took it back to the Green Bay 30," was just one of Leaming's gems that comes to mind. Leaming would give way to the rich baritone voice of John Facenda, who became a true golden voice as the voice of NFL Films. John was a news anchor and never called a game in person, yet his voice was synonymous with the NFL for more than two decades. The NFL had a 12-game season in those days. Not until 1961 did it jump to 14 games. Often there were six preseason games and very few, if any, were televised. There were no Monday night games, no Thursday night games, and no West Coast late games. Once in a while the Browns played a Saturday night game, but by and large college football was on Saturday and pro football on Sunday. The AFL's entrance into the picture in the early 1960s brought a second game to our TV screens with plenty of razzle-dazzle offense and crazy-looking uniforms. Slo-mo and instant replay were still a long way off, but it was football—fuzzy and in black and white. Primitive by today's standards.

About that time, in the early 1960s, my friend Steve Sturges discovered his parents' tape recorder. Steve began recording every important sports event of the period and some that were not so important. He focused especially on the

Browns, and together we would condense the games into a series of great Jimmy Brown runs and Frank Ryan pass plays. We mixed in the Rose Bowl with Mel Allen, the Army-Navy game with Lindsey Nelson, and the College All-Star Game with Curt Gowdy. It was at that time that the dream was formed to one day become a sports broadcaster myself.

The Golden Voices of Football salutes the pioneer broadcasters of yesteryear who broadcast from makeshift, unheated perches, especially in the early years, with just basic fragments of information, no color men, and primitive, unsophisticated spotting boards. Graham McNamee, Ted Husing, Quin Ryan, Ty Tyson, Tom Manning, Bill Munday, Harry Wismer, and Bill Stern blazed the trail for those who followed, such as Lindsey Nelson, Mel Allen, Curt Gowdy, Ray Scott, and Keith Jackson.

In radio's infancy, accuracy and knowledge of the game sometimes took a backseat to colorful descriptions and dramatic pauses. Graham McNamee talked more about the sunset at the Rose Bowl than the game itself. Bill Stern wouldn't give the score if the game was one-sided, and Harry Wismer talked more about his celebrity friends in the stands than the players in uniform.

Just a few years before I began my research, instant replay was introduced during the Army-Navy game in Philadelphia. CBS paid the astronomical sum of $28 million for the rights to NFL games in 1964. Now John Madden's contract with Rupert Murdoch and Fox exceeds that amount.

This book, following its predecessor, *The Golden Voices of Baseball*, attempts to chronicle the growth of football broadcasting, dissecting the characters and personalities of sportscasting's most memorable figures. The project began as an undergrad broadcasting project at the University of Dayton and continued at Miami University in Oxford, Ohio. Armed with a tape recorder and a dream, I canvassed the east and Midwest in search of pioneer sportscasters. I found Harry Wismer in a hospital bed in Port Huron, Michigan. Bill Stern was in his Mutual broadcasting studio in New York. Joe Tucker took me to a Pirates-Giants game at Forbes Field, while Howard Cosell tried to give me a crash course on broadcast journalism in his office at ABC. Tom Manning was winding down his long career in Cleveland, while Mel Allen was trying to reignite his career, which was drifting since the Yankees let him go in 1964. It took a week to track down Jim Britt in Boston while in Pittsburgh; my car was stolen while interviewing Mrs. Rosey Rowswell. Incredibly, I didn't have to go far to find the world's first sportscaster. Harold Arlin, who recorded all of the firsts at KDKA in Pittsburgh, was living just a block away in my hometown of Mansfield, Ohio.

My chief regret is that so many of the great broadcasters who graciously gave of their time, supplying taped interviews, photographs, and sincere support for this project, are not alive to see it finally reach fruition. But thanks to the magic of audio recordings, their voices and play-by-play calls are preserved forever, and in this volume not only can you read about the pioneer announcers and look at memorable photos of them in their prime, but you can listen to them, too. With a few exceptions, the criteria for being included among "The Golden Voices" was to have begun broadcasting either before or right after World War II. Thus, recognizable names such as Verne Lundquist, Al Michaels, Van Miller, Don Criqui, Rick Weaver, Bob Martin, and Brent Musberger have been regretfully omitted.

It's time for the kickoff as described by *The Golden Voices of Football.*

Photo courtesy of NBC

The Golden Voices
of Football

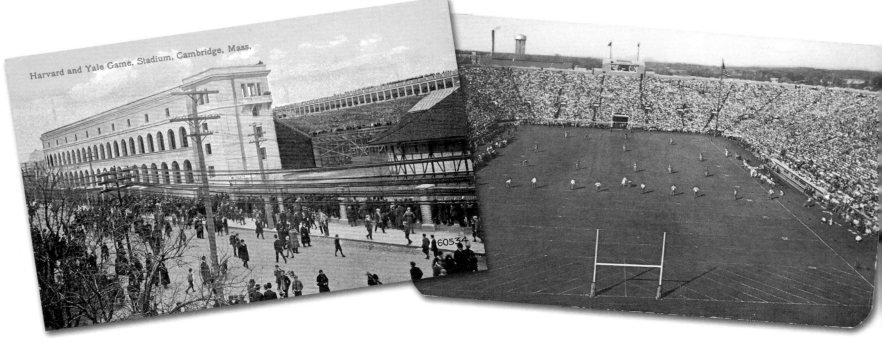

Golden Voices
from the Golden Age

AIR VIEW OF PHILADELPHIA MUNICIPAL STADIUM, SO. PHILADELPHIA, PA.   PH-12

122:—NEW UNIVERSITY OF PITTSBURGH STADIUM, PITTSBURGH, PA.

Aerial View of the Stadium, University of Notre Dame, Notre Dame, Indiana

© D. ROACH

9A-H848

STADIUM, OHIO STATE UNIVERSITY, COLUMBUS, OHIO

P-38   THE ROSE BOWL, PASADENA, CALIFORNIA

SPEN

6A-H1823

P-38   THE ROSE BOWL, TOURNAMENT OF ROSES STADIUM, PASADENA, CALIFORNIA

4559-29

What a marriage. Sports and broadcasting. First radio and then radio and television. They've been together for more than 80 years and are still acting like a couple of newlyweds. There was doubt at first. Several owners and executives believed that attendance at the games would shrink because the public would stay home and listen for free. But that myth was soon dispelled when crowd totals soared and the sports fans of the golden age went crazy over Jack Dempsey, Babe Ruth, Red Grange, and Bobby Jones.

Radio's heroes weren't so well known, but they shared stature with the athletes that they would glamorize over the airwaves. Guglielmo Marconi, Dr. Frank Conrad, Lee De Forest, Thomas Edison, and David Sarnoff all helped perfect the sending of wireless voice communications. Marconi was the Abner Doubleday of radio. He took the telegraphic code invented by Samuel Morse in the 1840s, removed the wires, and sent the first wireless messages in 1895. Moving from his native Italy to England in 1896, Marconi transmitted across the English Channel in 1899 and was transmitting across the Atlantic Ocean by 1901. He put together a makeshift antenna off the coast of Wales and another across the ocean in Newfoundland where he sent up balloons and kites that were fastened with wires. He sent three short dots—the letter S—and radio was on its way. Soon Marconi's inventions drew the interest

Red Grange would move from his career on the gridiron to one behind the mike.
Courtesy of the author's collection

of the U.S. government, and the equipment was installed on ships and lighthouses. Until wireless, pigeons had been the chief method of ship-to-shore communication.

Seizing upon Marconi's impetus, two American inventors made significant contributions in transmitting the human voice by wireless means. One was University of Pittsburgh professor Reginald Fessenden, and the other was a scholarly Yale grad named Lee De Forest. Fessenden was the first to think that there might be a way of transmitting musical notes and perhaps even the human voice

Italian inventor Guglielmo Marconi sends his first wireless radio transmission in America (above), Marconi (below) began the push that led to radio becoming a means of mass communication. *Background photo provided by the Museum of the City of New York/Byron Collection/Getty Images; foreground photo courtesy of NBC*

through the air. De Forest established the American Wireless Telegraphic Company in 1901 and began manufacturing sending and receiving sets for the government. In 1906 he invented the audion tube, another major breakthrough.

Fessenden thought he could superimpose the human voice on a flow of high frequency vibrations in the way Alexander Graham Bell had succeeded with sending the human voice on electric currents. With the help of a young technician in the Schenectady, New

Marconi (above) at work with wireless in 1920. Lee De Forest (below) poses with his technological contribution to radio, the electron tube. *Photos provided by Hulton Archive/Getty Images*

York, General Electric plant named Ernest Alexanderson, Fessenden developed a machine that could "speak." On Christmas Eve 1906 on the coast of Massachusetts from a 420-foot tower, they first sent the Morse code message—"CQ, CQ." Confused ships at sea were startled when they heard the sound of human voices spouting from their speakers. Interspersing musical solos with poem recitals, Fessenden and Alexanderson had succeeded in transmitting one of the first documented radio broadcasts.

In 1908 De Forest was playing phonograph records by wireless from the top of the Eiffel Tower. Four years later, a young immigrant from a Jewish section of the Russian province Minsk became an operator and manager of a station located atop the Wanamaker

Reginald Fessenden (left) theorized about transmitting sounds through the air. David Sarnoff and Marconi took advantage of these technological advances to create RCA and its radio network, NBC. *Drawing courtesy of the author's collection; photo courtesy of NBC*

department store in New York City. While sitting at the Wanamaker telegraph on April 14, 1912, the 22-year-old operator, David Sarnoff, took the first desperate messages from the *SS Olympic* 1,400 miles out at sea; *"SS Titanic* ran into iceberg. Sinking fast." For 72 hours the world stood still, waiting for the messages that clicked over his key. For Sarnoff it was the launching of a career that would lead him to become the chairman and founder of RCA and its radio offspring, NBC.

Talk about predictions that came to fruition. In 1904, an inventor named Nikola Tesla wrote of a mechanism that "will be very efficient in enlightening the masses, a cheap and simple device which might be carried in one's pocket." In 1916, Sarnoff prophesied a plan of development that would make radio a "household utility in the same sense as the piano or phonograph. The idea is to bring music into the home by wireless. The same principles can be extended to numerous other fields. Baseball scores can be

Air Concert "Picked Up" By Radio Here

Victrola music, played into the air over a wireless telephone, was "picked up" by listeners on the wireless receiving station which was recently installed here for patrons interested in wireless experiments. The concert was heard Thursday night about 10 o'clock, and continued 20 minutes. Two orchestra numbers, a soprano solo—which rang particularly high, and clear through the air—and a juvenile "talking piece" constituted the program.

The music was from a Victrola pulled up close to the transmitter of a wireless telephone in the home of Frank Conrad, Penn and Peebles avenues, Wilkinsburg. Mr. Conrad is a wireless enthusiast and "puts on" the wireless concerts periodically for the entertainment of the many people in this district who have wireless sets.

Amateur Wireless Sets, made by the maker of the Set which is in operation in our store, are on sale here $10.00 up.

—West Basement

transmitted in the air by the use of one set installed at the Polo Grounds."

Few were convinced by Sarnoff's prophecy. He couldn't even convince those in his own business of radio's possibilities, much less the general public.

World War I speeded up radio's development. Radio served as a mechanical spy in stealing enemy messages. It was installed in airplanes so that squadron commanders could communicate with their pilots. It became essential in all naval vessels. The navy became the prime controller of radio as great technical strides were made. At war's end, the Radio Corporation of

Sarnoff (left) predicted radio's popularity with the American public. This ad marks one of Dr. Frank Conrad's early broadcasts on 8XK in Pittsburgh. *Photo courtesy of NBC; clipping courtesy of News/Talk 1020, KDKA, Pittsburgh*

America was born on December 1, 1919, with David Sarnoff as its leader. Interfering stations, both amateur and commercial, were creating havoc by jumbling frequencies. The Department of Commerce was forced to allot wavelengths and control their use.

Dr. Frank Conrad, experimenting on his home radio station 8XK in Pittsburgh, became radio's first disc jockey. A phonograph produced the music, and Conrad interjected the needed talk. When his supply of records dwindled, a music store gave him records in exchange for commercial plugs. On September 29, 1920, a newspaper ad told how a receiving station installed in the basement of Horn's department store had picked up a concert sent out by Conrad. Conrad's widow said upon his death in 1941, "Nobody could ever appreciate the hours he labored unless one was there to witness it. It grew from just a few wires wrapped around a piece of pipe with little legs extending from the tube. I just couldn't believe it when I stared at that monstrosity and it talked back to me."

Unbeknownst to Conrad, Westinghouse Vice President H.P. Davis was following his ventures with interest. Davis, with his powerful company behind him, built a larger transmitting station to see just what radio could do. A commercial license application was submitted on October 16, 1920, and the presidential election returns of November 2, 1920, became radio's first official broadcast. Radio almost unconsciously passed into broadcasting.

Other stations soon began popping up. On October 1, 1921, Westinghouse station WJZ began operating from a factory roof in Newark, New Jersey, as pioneer announcer Thomas H. Cowan helped inaugurate broadcasting in the east. Westinghouse also opened stations in Springfield, Massachusetts—WBZ—and in Chicago—KYW. Station WHK, Cleveland's first commercial station, began operation in 1921.

On Washington's birthday, February 22, 1922, in a windowless corner on the top floor of the L. Bamberger department store in Newark, New Jersey, station WOR was born, as a record of Al Jolson's *April Showers* was played. Boston's first radio station, WNAC, went on the air July 31, 1922, with 100 watts of power and an antenna on the roof supported by a clothesline. On August 16, 1922, station WEAF in New York signed on for the first time. Financed and constructed by AT&T, WEAF, which later became WNBC, was one of the first stations to broadcast on a continuous programming basis and to sell advertising, something that rankled inventor Lee De Forest. He complained, "What have you done with my child?" he screamed after commercials became commonplace. "You have made of him a laughingstock of intelligence, surely a stench in the nostrils of the gods of the ionosphere."

By the early 1920s the entire nation was flocking to buy radio sets. The number of stations rose from three in August 1921 to 30 at the end of the year and then to 200 by the end of 1922. By the end of the decade, more than 618 stations were operating. At the end of World War I, people thought of wireless as they thought of dirigible airships—something modern and intriguing but with no direct bearing on ordinary life. Then homemade aerials, made from all kinds of metal including bedsprings, began sprouting up on people's rooftops. Every home wanted a radio, and for a while, radio apparatus became as hard to buy as sugar in wartime. "You can hear music from the air," became a popular phrase of the times. Farmers especially loved

9

the new device. "God bless radio," wrote one farmer's wife. "I have spent practically all my life within the four walls of my kitchen, but I can now hear something from the outer world, not only once a week or once a month, but nearly every hour of the day if I choose." William H. Easton wrote in *The New York Times* on April 1922: "What the printed page is to the eye, this device will be to the ear; and when, as may happen, it is combined with the radio moving picture, enabling anyone to see as well as hear what is going on in distant points, we shall have something that will probably revolutionize society."

Sports and radio were bonded together in ads (above) as radio grew in popularity as a contemporary means to stay informed and relax (left). *Ad courtesy of the author's collection; photo provided by the Hulton Archive/Getty Images*

With having to fill countless hours with some form of programming, it was only a matter of time before the radio stations got around to sports. Who aired the first sports broadcast is open to debate. KDKA, because it was the first licensed station, claims it was the first with the airing of a prizefight from the Pittsburgh Motor Gardens on April 11, 1921. However, as early as 1912, an attempt was made to broadcast football games by using a spark transmitter and regular telegraphic signals by the University of Minnesota experimental radio station. There is also documentation that on Thanksgiving Day in 1921, the Texas-Texas A&M game was broadcast from College Station by two Aggie cadets, W.A. Tolson and Harry Saunders. The wireless account was broadcast over station 5XB in College Station to station 5XU in Austin. In Austin, waiting for the transmission were W.E. Gray, C.C. Clark, and Werner Dornberger. Other amateur operators in Texas picked up the account, which was also used by the *Austin American* newspaper as a source of game information. Texas was favored to win the 1921 meeting between the two rivals, but the Aggies held them to a 0–0 tie.

A *Pittsburgh Post* sportswriter is given credit for broadcasting the first sports event. It happened on April 11, 1921, in the Motor Gardens when Florent Gibson of the *Pittsburgh Post* broadcast the Johnny Ray-Johnny Dundee featherweight bout. Ray clearly out-boxed Dundee in 10 rounds. In a separate article, the *Post* talked about Gibson's broadcast and how "countless fight fans received the news of each blow struck and each bit of ring strategy enacted the instant it occurred."

In 1970 Gibson was still working for the paper on the copy desk at age 82. Gibson had led a colorful life. Born in West Virginia and raised in Big Prairie, Ohio, near Canton, Gibson played football at Denison University until a serious leg injury forced him to the sidelines. He joined the *Post* in June 1912 as a temporary replacement and was still there 68 years later. During his lunch hour at the paper, Gibson

Florent Gibson broadcast the first sports event, a boxing match between Johnny Ray and Johnny Dundee in 1921. *Photo courtesy of the* **Pittsburgh Post-Gazette**

Harold Arlin (right) became radio's first full-time announcer in 1921. Arlin (below) and Tom Bender commemorate the 45th anniversary of the first college football broadcast, which was announced by Arlin. *Photos courtesy of News/Talk 1020, KDKA, Pittsburgh*

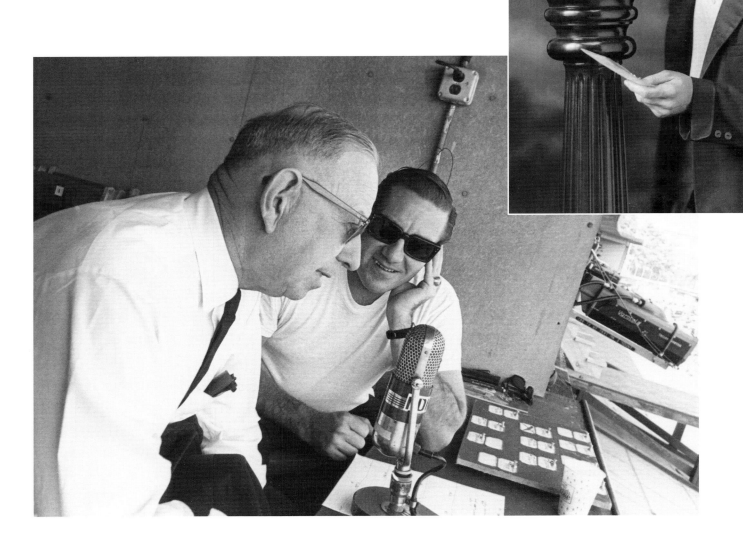

wrestled in a Pittsburgh burlesque house under the name of "The Masked Marvel." Gibson broadcast several more events on KDKA, including the November 11, 1921, fight at the Motor Gardens between Harry Greb, the "Pittsburgh Windmill," and Billy Shade of Australia. In 1924 he was asked to do the blow by blow of the Harry Wills-Luis Firpo fight from Boyle's Thirty Acres in Jersey City, New Jersey, back to Firpo's home country of Argentina. "Funny part of it was that up beyond the Artic Circle there was a group of Spanish explorers who also heard the fight," remembered Gibson. "There was one man who translated my description into Spanish, so I broadcast the fight north in Spanish and south in English."

Gibson formed some definite opinions about radio and television. "Television is a curse," he was quick to say. "Kids watch it more hours than they spend in school. Maybe I'm just a prejudiced old fogey, but I did have something to do with the start of radio, God forgive me." Florent Gibson died on March 1, 1976, at age 88.

But Gibson gets short shrift when the roll call of early sports announcers is read. The July 2, 1921, bout between heavyweight champion Jack Dempsey and challenger Georges Carpentier, the Orchid man of France, at Boyle's Thirty Acres in Hoboken, New Jersey, is regarded in most history books as the first boxing match broadcast. David Sarnoff was upset that KDKA and Westinghouse had gotten the jump on his RCA factory for early broadcasting prestige. The bout was billed as "The Battle of the Century," and Sarnoff was determined to broadcast it. He went to J. Andrew White, the editor of *Wireless Age* magazine with the idea. The trouble was RCA had no radio stations and neither did Sarnoff or White. So they constructed their own. White was the announcer in the fight, which

ended with a Dempsey fourth-round knockout. Technically, a bout on the preliminary card was broadcast first. White was testing the line during the latter rounds of the Packey O'Gatty-Frankie Burns eight-round bout. A slight drizzle began falling in the sixth round, and White, concerned that the main event might be called off, began reporting the blow by blow of the two featherweights. Promoter Tex Richard then told White to announce that the main event would be staged rain or shine.

Some 300,000 people in clubs, halls, and theaters as well as in their homes heard the fight, some from as far as 500 miles away. One 15-year-old boy erected a homemade wireless outfit in his Hackensack backyard out of waste wood and pieces of wire. On the night of July 1 he ran inside and told his father he heard somebody speaking. His father scoffed at first until hearing the voices himself. The father could only say that if an amateurish, primitive, wireless outfit assembled by a schoolboy could receive messages so distinctly, it certainly seemed that radio had a bright future. The news of what a Reuter's official called "the world's first real broadcast," was reported throughout Europe. Radio announcer White wrote in the next issue of his *Wireless Age* magazine: "Describing the big scrap was the toughest reporting job I ever tackled. Jammed up against the ring in a little coop without elbow room and with bedlam breaking lose on every side, it's a wonder it sounded intelligible. The men punched quicker than could be noted by speech. Their speed baffled the tongue; even the eye was strained. I could only give the highlight punches—the ones that did some damage."

Meanwhile, back in Pittsburgh, Westinghouse Vice President H.P. Davis was building a broadcasting studio for his KDKA outlet. Davis remarked a few years later, "[W]e were convinced that we had in our hands the instrument that would prove to be the greatest and most direct mass communicational means ever devised. The natural fascination of its mystery, coupled with its ability to annihilate distance, would attract interest and open many avenues to bring ease and happiness into human lives."

It was this mystery that caused a young Westinghouse foreman named Harold Arlin to see his life course change as radio's first full-time announcer. The 26-year-old from tiny LaHarpe, Illinois, had graduated from the University of Kansas in 1917. He watched the Kansas football team on Saturday afternoons, never thinking that he would one day broadcast the first college football game in radio history. Or that he would have a football field named after him in his adopted hometown of Mansfield, Ohio. Arlin had been working in the Westinghouse plant as a time-study foreman and wandered up to the rooftop radio station out of curiosity. He soon found himself slipping into a tuxedo and hosting dance band remotes, speeches, and other activities as KDKA's first announcer.

On August 4, 1921, Arlin broadcast Davis Cup tennis matches with Australia beating Great Britain at Pittsburgh's Allegheny Country Club, and it was on Saturday, August 5 that Arlin broadcast the first baseball game on radio as the Pirates beat the Phillies 8-5 at Forbes Field.

The University of Pittsburgh football program had been on the rise ever since Glenn "Pop" Warner took over as coach in 1915 after a highly successful tenure at the Carlisle School for Indians where he coached the legendary Jim Thorpe. His first year at Pitt saw the

Panthers go unbeaten, posting five shutouts and outscoring the opposition 247 points to 47. The following year he did even better, going unbeaten with a scoring margin of 255 to 25, with just Carnegie Tech and Navy scoring points against them. World War I didn't stop Pops's Panthers, who were led by Jock Sutherland, who eventually replaced Warner as coach. Pitt was 9-0 in 1917, outscoring the opposition 231 points to 15. The Panthers were in a golden era, winning 40 straight games before Syracuse snapped the streak in the third game of the 1919 season.

By the time the 1921 season rolled around, Warner had lost just two games in six seasons. His teams were nationally ranked, and it was only natural, with all the interest surrounding the team, that KDKA would decide to broadcast a game. Warner's "Men of Steel" hosted traditional rival West Virginia on October 8. Arlin drew the assignment, and behind the play of All-Americans Tom Davies and Herb Stein, Pitt defeated the Mountaineers 21-14. Arlin's microphone that day was shaped like a round metal oatmeal box and lined with felt to filter out the noises from the field.

Arlin's second football broadcast became a more vivid memory for several reasons. The opponent was Nebraska, and it was the first time the Cornhuskers came east to play. Pitt was a heavy favorite, but Arlin remembered from his Kansas days how competitive Nebraska was in the tough Missouri Valley conference. The score was 0-0 at halftime. "Nebraska had an All-America end by the name of C.E. Swanson and a halfback named Hartley," remembered Arlin several decades later, "and when Hartley took a pitchout and tossed a long touchdown pass to Swanson, I got so excited and yelled so loudly that the modulation meter broke on the transmitter, blowing the station off the air." The next day's newspaper commented on KDKA's modulation mishap: "'Nebraska is over for a touchdown!' the announcer shrieked into the microphone. Then silence. Listeners shook their earphones and tinkered with their crystal sets. Five minutes passed and as mysteriously as it had stopped, the broadcast began again. Just one of the expected hazards as radio cuts its teeth on broadcasting college football." As a result of the incident, a backup circuit was installed for emergencies. "Necessity was the mother of invention in those days," added Arlin. Nebraska, by the way, defeated Pitt 10-0 in a huge upset.

Arlin, called by *The New York Times*, "the best known American voice in Europe," departed broadcasting just five years after he had begun, taking a job in industrial relations at the Westinghouse plant in Mansfield, Ohio. It was there that he raised his family, becoming a civic leader and having the 12,000-seat high school football stadium—Arlin Field—named in his honor. He returned to Pittsburgh for anniversaries of his baseball and football broadcasts and spent his latter years following the pitching exploits of his grandson, Steve Arlin. Harold Arlin passed away on March 14, 1986, at age 90.

Like Arlin in Pittsburgh, a Westinghouse plant also employed Tommy Cowan. He worked in the Newark, New Jersey, facility and became the pioneer announcer of WJZ, the first station in the East, putting the station on the air in September 1921. He was the first announcer in the New York metropolitan area. With a formal education that ended at age 14, Cowan worked as an office boy for *The New York World* and then joined the Edison Laboratory in West Orange, New Jersey.

Boxer Jack Dempsey listens to a radio tuned by J. Andrew White before the Dempsey-Carpentier fight in 1921. *Photo courtesy of NBC*

"You have no idea how little your own time meant to you, until you got into radio," remembered Cowan in August 1969, just two and a half months before his death at age 85. "Every breath you took seemed to belong to somebody else, and everybody was on their toes thinking the whole thing was going to blow up. Radio was made to order for me because I was a very morbid kid. I always wanted to be a great singer, and I couldn't sing any better than a car wanting to get into the door."

Cowan played phonograph records because they couldn't afford to pay an entertainer for a live performance. Orchestra leader Vincent Lopez, then playing at the Pennsylvania Grill in New York, was asked by Cowan to fill in one Sunday evening. Lopez was extremely nervous, as he wrote in his autobiography: "I'll never forget Tommy Cowan turning to me and saying, 'Vincent, why don't you announce the program?' Me, announce the program? Tommy and I argued the point for a few minutes. When the program began, I stepped up on a little platform and said, 'Hello, everybody, Lopez speaking.' Cowan jumped up alongside me and said, 'Is that all you're going to say, Mr. Lopez?' 'That's enough for me,' I answered." It was the first appearance of a live dance band on radio. Also the first

> **"You have no idea how little your own time meant to you, until you got into radio, every breath you took seemed to belong to somebody else, and everybody was on their toes thinking the whole thing was going to blow up."** —Tommy Cowan

to introduce Ed Wynn and the Perfect Fool on radio, Cowan also helped relay Grantland Rice's telephone play by play during the 1921 World Series, broadcasting half-inning recaps on KDKA, WJZ, and WBZ. In 1925, Cowan became chief announcer at WNYC and remained on the job until his retirement 36 years later. Mayor Jimmy Walker proclaimed him New York's "official greeter," a position he held for several decades under several different mayors, including Fiorello LaGuardia. Cowan also had a hand in the broadcast of two important boxing events in the early 1920s. The first on June 26, 1922, pitted champion Jack Britton and challenger Benny Leonard from New York's Velodrome. It was the first event ever broadcast that was not telephoned back to the originating station before it was sent out. Cowan introduced J. Andrew White, who did the blow by blow of a controversial decision in which Leonard struck Britton in the 13th round while he was down and was disqualified. On July 27, 1922, Cowan again introduced the festivities as Leonard fought southpaw challenger Lew Tendler at Boyle's Thirty Acres. Leonard defended his lightweight title, and along Broadway, crowds of people listened to giant loudspeakers reporting the fight. This bout clinched radio as a successful means of transmitting

Robert "Buz" Kingensmith (right), shown here with boxer Billy Conn, broadcast the first high school football game. *Photo courtesy of the author's collection*

sports events. Said one observer: "In the future, no sporting event of major importance will be complete without it." Cowan remained with WNYC until 1961, when failing eyesight forced him to retire.

In many cases, such as in J. Andrew White handling the fights, sportswriters were recruited to broadcast sports events. In the 1922 World Series between the Yankees and Giants, legendary sportswriter Grantland Rice teamed with fellow writer W.O. "Bill" McGheehan to describe the action. People without radio sets flocked to radio stores to hear the series. Rice wrote of the experience, "It was as simple as talking to one man, a dumb man who isn't deaf, as simple as asking for a cigarette or ordering a peck of potatoes from the grocer over the phone. The most intricate contrivance in the world, to one as unversed in mechanics or electricity as we are, had suddenly become the simplest thing in a highly complex age."

Immediately following the World Series broadcast, WJZ began broadcasting the fall collegiate football season, opening with the game between host Princeton and Colgate. The game was broadcast by telegraph and relayed to the public after the code was disseminated. On October 21, 1922, the Fordham-Georgetown game was broadcast direct from the Polo Grounds with the radio audience being able to hear the cheering and the school songs of the students as well as the description of the game from the press box. On October 28, Syracuse versus Penn State was broadcast from the Polo Grounds, followed by the November 4 WJZ broadcast of the Lafayette College-Washington and Jefferson game. Then came Cornell-Dartmouth and the Army-Navy game of November 25, 1922, from Philadelphia.

On October 28, 1922, New York station WEAF broadcast the first college football game heard coast to coast. Princeton played the University of Chicago at Stagg Field in the Windy City. The broadcast was carried on phone lines to New York City, where the transmission began. Princeton edged the Maroons 21-18.

Technicians at WDAP, which became WGN, used a five-watt transmitter
from component parts to broadcast. *Photo courtesy of WGN Radio*

Sportswriter Robert "Buz" Klingensmith broadcast the first high school sporting event on KDKA on December 9, 1921, as state power Wilkinsburg played Washington High School at Forbes Field for the state championship. Wilkinsburg defeated Washington 7-6. "It was a bitterly cold day, and the schools' band instruments froze," Klingensmith remembered. "As an announcer, I was a loudmouth. Haven't they all been? I later wrote the game story, never once referring to the fact that I had broadcast it on radio. It was not an historic occasion, and, in fact, I thought it unwise to be

identified with it, although the station introduced me. After all, radio was just a toy at the time. Then came the response. A grandmother of one of the players said she listened and was thrilled to hear about the good game played by her grandson. Cards were received, referring primarily to reception and not the game or the announcer."

Other firsts in the world of sports broadcasting were tabulated as the decade of the 1920s progressed. Station WNAC in Boston aired the first college baseball game at Harvard in 1922. KHJ in Los Angeles broadcast the first Rose Bowl in the L.A. area. WNAC also broadcast the first golf tournament on April 4, 1926, and did one of the first hockey games in the East, a Canadian-American Hockey League game on December 10, 1926. Polo was broadcast for the first time on September 12, 1923, as the championship game at the Meadowbrook Club was broadcast by WJZ. J. Andrew White described the first horse race, between Zev and Epinard from Belmont Park on WJZ on September 1, 1924.

Although KDKA was the nation's first licensed station, WGN in Chicago soon surpassed it in its depth of sports coverage, and announcer Quin Ryan took the impetus from Arlin in Pittsburgh to become the Midwest's most prolific early broadcaster. WGN was called WDAP in its infancy. A.W. "Sen" Kaney broadcast the Indianapolis 500 Memorial Day race in 1924 on WDAP. Two automotive greats, driver Barney Oldfield and carmaker Henry Ford spoke into the WDAP microphone. By late summer of that year, when radio covered anything that made noise, Ryan came aboard to launch a spectacular career in radio. Ryan had been attending classes at Northwestern where he dabbled in acting, wrote columns, and was a cub reporter, ghostwriter, and freelance announcer. He was also working for the *Chicago Tribune* in his spare time. One of Quin's first assignments was reading the Sunday comic strips as Uncle Quin, something he would do for 17 straight years. With the state of Illinois in a frenzy over the gridiron exploits of the fabled "Galloping Ghost," Red Grange at the University of Illinois, Ryan convinced the station management to broadcast the Illinois-Michigan game on October 18, 1924, that also saw the new Memorial Stadium

dedicated before a capacity crowd of more than 67,000 fans. Grange didn't disappoint. "The Wheaton Iceman" scored four touchdowns in the first quarter as the Illini won 39-14. Ryan didn't disappoint, either. Without the luxury of a radio booth, he sat up on the roof of the press box, reveling with delight in his "Gee Whiz" style that the Illini came on the field bare legged without socks (a first for Illinois), and that Grange's number 77 was the same number as the Michigan fans' special train, meaning in other words, Red had Michigan's number from the get-go. ("Telegrams came into the studio claiming I was crazy that every time Grange got his hands on the ball, I thought it was a score.")

By this time there were more than 100,000 receiving sets in the Chicago area, and most were tuned to Ryan and WGN. Like Graham McNamee who followed him on the network level, Quin Ryan became Mr. Versatility, adept at handling any assignment. He began broadcasting the home games of the Cubs and White Sox and was the first man to recreate baseball game from wire reports. In fact, he designed the concept and even recreated memorable events such as the 1871 Chicago fire from news reports.

On New Year's Day in 1925, Ryan sat in frigid Chicago at the station's Drake Hotel studio and broadcast by telegraphic code the Tournament of Roses Parade and followed that with a ticker-tape description of the Rose Bowl football game in Pasadena as Notre Dame's fabled Four Horsemen ended their careers with a 27-10 win over Ernie Nevers's Stanford Indians. The station hired a band and invited a flock of alumni and cheerleaders to keep Quin company during the broadcast.

Next on the sports lineup was the 1925 Kentucky Derby in Louisville, where Ryan reported from the cupola above the stands at Churchill Downs. Often he would team with a couple of young comedians on the station, Freeman Gosden and Charles Correll, who first called themselves Sam 'n' Henry and then became the beloved Amos 'n' Andy. A few weeks later, on Memorial Day in 1925, Ryan broadcast the Indianapolis 500, which was on the air for seven hours, and then in July 1925, in a stifling-hot Dayton, Tennessee, courtroom, Ryan anchored the WGN broadcast of the famous Scopes Monkey evolution trial, which pitted William Jennings Bryan against defense attorney Clarence Darrow. There were more than 200 newspapermen covering the trial, but only one sent the story out over the airwaves. Quin described how Scopes was found guilty and fined $100. Five days later Bryan died of apoplexy at age 65. In the 1960 Stanley Kramer movie *Inherit The Wind*, Frederick March played Ryan, squaring off with Spencer Tracy who portrayed Darrow. Dick York played Scopes, and dancer-actor Gene Kelly played caustic columnist H.L. Mencken.

Quin Ryan (above, far right) was a versatile broadcaster covering the Republican Convention and interviewing University of Illinois star Red Grange (below). *Photos courtesy of WGN Radio*

Quin Ryan interviews Sydney Smith, the creator of *The Gumps*, in 1924. **Photo courtesy of WGN Radio**

Ryan as the 1925 college football season commenced. For one thing, he was in a glass-enclosed cubicle, and for another, a "spotter" was provided to identify players. In 1932, WGN ambitiously broadcast a football game from Los Angeles, which was the longest remote by a single radio station up to that time. It prompted a new slogan: "The station that broadcasts FROM greater distances than others broadcast TO."

Ryan was still logging firsts as late as 1941. It was during that year's football season that WGN broadcast the referees' pregame and coin-flip ceremonies at midfield of the Northwestern-Michigan game. Quin was holding the microphone, and wearing a trench coat that had WGN on its back. "In my lucky career of doing many of the nation's first coast-to-coast sporting events," Quin said, "my microphone scooped up and bounced more deafening racket into more ears than anything in history prior to World War II and the atom bomb. During that first decade we accepted no sponsorships and gave the audience the whole day's show."

In October 1925, baseball commissioner Judge Mountain Landis picked Quin, along with a young tenor-turned-broadcaster named Graham McNamee to broadcast the first coast-to-coast hookup of the World Series between the Pirates and Senators. The network comprised two legs or chains, one originating in New York and the other in Chicago. There were no sponsorships. "Mac and I changed 'legs' each day, alternating between the east and west chains," remembered Quin. Things improved dramatically for

Quin Ryan (third from right) interviews George Ade, a writer and humorist, while Purdue president E.C. Elliott (far left) and Indiana governor Happy Leslie (second from left) look on during halftime at the Purdue-Wisconsin game on October 25, 1930.
Photo courtesy of WGN Radio

Notre Dame's Four Horsemen (from left to right) Don Miller, Elmer Layden, Jim Crowley, and Harry Stuhldreher ended their careers at the Rose Bowl in 1925, which was broadcast by Quin Ryan. ***Photo provided by Hulton Archive/Getty Images***

Unlike Harold Arlin, who left broadcasting after five years, Ryan loved the business and made it his life's work. From political conventions to sailboat races, from daily Cubs and White Sox broadcasts to 17 seasons of college football, Ryan was behind the microphone. Quin even broadcast Knute Rockne's funeral in South Bend in 1931. "Quin Ryan was the father of sports broadcasting," said Ronald Reagan, who began his multifaceted career as a sports announcer. "It was Quin Ryan who got the idea that

you could sit and describe a football game and make someone else see it. In just a few years, Quin had created a profession."

Ryan remembered when Slip Madigan brought his St. Mary's football team to Soldier Field to play a Friday night game with Marquette. During the game, the sound of the vendors could be heard over Ryan's mike. Listeners began wiring telegrams to Quin about the state of affairs. He read some of the messages over the air, whereupon a spectator, who was equipped with a

Thousands of fans listen to Quin Ryan broadcast the memorial service of Knute Rockne, Notre Dame's famed coach, in 1931 because there wasn't enough room in the South Bend Church of the Sacred Heart. *Photo provided by the Chicago Tribune*

portable radio, raced to the public address microphone. "Attention all Catholics," he screamed. "It's Friday night!" More than 20,000 hot dogs went uneaten.

Quin handpicked two of his successors on WGN, Bob Elson and later Jack Brickhouse. He became general manager of the station in 1930 and served in that capacity for 10 years. For a long time he was a radio-TV columnist in the *Tribune*. Quin Ryan, broadcasting pioneer of the highest magnitude, passed away on October 7, 1978. He was 79 years old.

Radio Age magazine conducted the first radio popularity poll in September 1924, with "The Solemn Old Judge," George Hay, winning top honors. Second in popularity was a young tenor working at WEAF in New York named Graham McNamee. Harold Arlin of KDKA was fourth. Listeners were becoming more and more aware of whom and what they were listening to as the initial novelty of radio was wearing off. In the field of sports broadcasting on the network level, McNamee, Ted Husing, and Bill Munday became college football's top voices. They quickly became known as "The Big Three."

WGN broadcasts the first pregame instructions on October 19, 1941, at the Northwestern-Michigan game. Ryan is in the WGN raincoat. *Photo provided by the Chicago Tribune*

The Big Three

Bill Munday

Ted Husing

Graham McNamee

*Munday photo courtesy of the University of Georgia;
Husing and McNamee photos courtesy of NBC*

In radio's infancy, versatility was the key ingredient that separated the good announcers from the great ones. The more well versed a broadcaster was on a variety of subjects, the more valuable he became, because assignments varied from day to day. There might be a dance band remote one night and a political speech the next. Setting the standard in radio's early years was Graham McNamee. Enthusiastic, vibrant, and blessed with an excitable, resonant delivery, the former singing tenor joined NBC in 1923 and soon became its biggest star.

Whether it be a heavyweight title fight or a political convention, it was breathtaking when McNamee was on the air. He, more than anyone else, blazed the trail on a network level for broadcasting's first 20 years. For example, he would fly to Los Angeles for a football broadcast and return the following day to New York to appear on Ed Wynn's Texaco program. The following night he might be seated at ringside, preparing to broadcast a major prizefight. No president could be inaugurated nor a heavyweight champion crowned without McNamee's presence.

Born in Washington, D.C. in 1889, the McNamee family moved a few years later to Minneapolis-St. Paul where Graham began studying music, which he hoped would lead to a career as a singer. In the early 1920s he headed for New York to try to make it big. Instead he found himself singing in churches for little or no remuneration. He volunteered for jury duty at three dollars a day and on a break one day between trials, he wandered into the studios of WEAF. He knew singers were on radio and was curious to see what broadcasting was all about. Within an hour his life had

Graham McNamee's (right) command of the mike set the tone and style of network radio. Famed writer Westbrook Pegler is on McNamee's right. *Photo courtesy of NBC*

Track 6

changed, as program director Sam Ross was impressed with Graham's voice as well as his personality and gave him an audition followed by a job offer. Thinking radio wouldn't last, McNamee took the job to make some money until the concert season began. As it turned out, his career as a singer was over.

McNamee's first sports broadcast was the Polo Grounds boxing match between middleweight champion Johnny Wilson and challenger Harry Greb. Greb won the fight, taking 13 of the 15 rounds, leaving in his wake a former middleweight champion with a large cut on his nose, a bleeding and torn mouth, puffed and raw lips, an almost-closed left eye, and a lump under his right eye.

Then came the 1923 World Series between the Yankees and Giants. McNamee played second banana to sportswriter W.O. "Bill" McGheehan, who hated the announcing job and gave it up in disgust in the fourth inning of the third game. Unlike the rapid-fire action of the Greb-Wilson fight, McNamee used his imagination due to the slower pace of the game. One of McNamee's top thrills came in Game Six with the Yankees leading in games 3-2. The Giants clung to a 4-3 seventh-inning lead when Babe Ruth came to bat with the bases loaded in the seventh inning. "Here was the most advertised athlete in the game, one whose name appears in headlines more often than the president's. One solid

McNamee in 1936. *Photo courtesy of NBC*

connection between bat and ball, and the series would be over. The chance that was the immortal Casey's was now the Babe's. Almost too engrossed to speak, I watched him as he came forward. He squared his shoulders and set himself menacingly enough—set himself and swung and missed. I never saw a more vicious swing." Two more swings later, and the poor Babe was out.

McNamee said he noticed in the series that he was getting further away from mere announcing and deeper into the reporter's realm—"To the voice qualifications, a sense of order; the ability to harmonize, synchronize, be on time, and let the reportorial instinct take over."

McNamee soon realized the marked difference between the sportswriter and the sports broadcaster. "Although some of the writer's work must be done in haste and on the spot, he still has time to absorb, to let impressions sink in, and he isn't bothered with having to talk all the time. After an event we do not have such vivid memories as the newspaper reporter or the most observant spectators." After the 1923 World Series, won by the Yankees in six games, their first of 20 in the next 40 years, McNamee received loads of mail, most of it positive, but a few naysayers protested his personal injections. "What do we care," they wrote, "whether you are cold or hot, wet or dry, or what's the state of your health! All we want to hear about is the game."

McNamee's longtime cohort Phillips Carlin, who became Graham's mike mate for countless events, was hired by WEAF a month after the 1923 World Series. Carlin had a great voice but wasn't adept in the music realm, which was an announcing prerequisite in the early years of radio. Carlin was a boyhood orator in school and worked in the silk business before joining WEAF as McNamee's sidekick. He later became program director and station manager.

"Good evening, ladies and gentlemen of the radio audience," became McNamee's trademark phrase as he greeted listeners. Sometimes he said it under duress, like his first football broadcast in the fall of 1923. During the first quarter it began pouring rain. Mac was broadcasting from a seat among the spectators along the sidelines, getting wetter by the minute. His one consideration, true to his profession and obligation, was to his carbon microphone. He knew that thousands of listeners were depending on him, so he took off his coat and wrapped it around the mike for protection. There were no broadcasting booths in those days, and radio wasn't important enough to warrant a place in the press box.

Listeners were becoming more particular and critical of McNamee, who was not renowned for his reportorial ability. It was the timbre in his voice and keen relish for spectacle that endeared him to the masses. For McNamee, a big football game wasn't just a job to do. He thrilled to the broken field runs, long kicks, do-or-die plays, and the listeners thrilled with him. He followed no rules. His "wows" and "whees" and exclamations of wonder and amazement punctuated his running descriptions.

At the Army-Navy game of 1925, played at the Polo Grounds, McNamee and Carlin chose a unique spot to broadcast from, the area in back of the baseball scoreboard. On a running board a few feet wide and 40 feet long they stood, placing the microphone in one of the little windows through which the score boys placed the run markers in the baseball season. As it turned out, they were at least sheltered from the bitter cold that the box seat patrons were experiencing.

The 1925 college football season provided McNamee with two of his great football broadcasting thrills: "Light Horse" Harry Wilson's 80-yard touchdown run in the Army-Yale game and Jake Slagel's 84-yard run in a game between Yale and Princeton. Both occurred at the Yale Bowl. "Slagel's was more spectacular," McNamee recalled, "because he ran through the entire team. Slagel took the ball and disappeared somewhere in the line. Then he eluded them one by one, straight-arming some and dodging others. Then, reversing his field, he finally got clear of all but one Yale tackler, who he outran to the end zone. He looked back over his shoulder at his pursuer several times and that worried movement added a wonderful thrill of suspense for the watching spectators."

Graham was the first to take the nation to the Rose Bowl, in 1927, after the NBC network was formed in November 1926. He broadcast the first coast-to-coast hookup, which required 4,000 miles of wire, leaving the audience limp with the thrills of a 7-7 tie between Alabama and Stanford. It was the Pitt-Stanford Rose Bowl of 1928 that really helped to build the McNamee

legend. He was overcome by the breathtaking sunset and the Sierra Madres, the awe-inspiring "Purple Mountains." United Press International dispatched this report: "Radio followers, shut in by ice blizzards along the Atlantic seaboard, sat intrigued by their firesides as they listened to details of the pageantry and the game, a striking contrast to the snowbound east and Midwest." Humorist Will Rogers added: "When somebody made a touchdown, Graham immediately told of the wondrous scenic beauty and the color of the roses on the Beverly Hills float in the Tournament's parade. I still don't know who made the touchdowns. And I'm not even certain of the score."

Accuracy was not one of McNamee's strengths. Like Bill Stern who would follow him, drama and descriptive storytelling were more important than reporting the game as it happened. When Roy Riegals made his famous wrong-way run in the 1929 Rose Bowl between California and Georgia Tech, McNamee seemed more perplexed than anyone in the stadium. He was doing the game with the third member of the early "Big Three," Bill Munday, on the biggest radio hookup put together at the time. When Georgia Tech's Stumpy Thomason fumbled and a

> **"You reach a point as you grow older when a football game simply can't become the most important thing in the world. When that time comes, you can't get up the same old excitement in your broadcast. Younger men must take over."**
>
> —Graham McNamee

confused Riegals scooped up the ball and headed in the wrong direction for his own goal line, McNamee was barely paying attention. Harlan Hall, the man who gave the Rose Bowl its name and sitting next to Graham shouted, "Boy, will this make football history!" Graham, as unaware as Riegals on what was happening on the field, stared at Hall with a puzzled look and naively asked, "Why?"

"Mac had spunk," recalled his old boss at NBC, John F. Royal. The legendary program director of radio's golden age said, "Graham was a very important man. He did a commercial once and said something in a political vein. Herbert Hoover, who was staying at the Waldorf, complained about it, and I had to go over and calm him down. He was more concerned about what McNamee said than another politician, because he knew the power that Graham wielded. Nobody ever reached the peak he achieved in radio."

McNamee's most memorable broadcast was the famed Jack Dempsey-Gene Tunney "long-count" fight at Soldier Field in Chicago on September 22, 1927. The largest network of stations in radio history were tuned in, the audience estimated at 50 million. McNamee ranked the "Long Count" bout his greatest sports thrill. Another was Albie Booth's play in the 1929 Yale-Army game at the Yale Bowl, which resulted in an Eli upset win.

FIFTEEN CENTS · October 3, 1927

TIME

The Weekly Newsmagazine

GRAHAM McNAMEE
He has many happy returns
(See Sport)

Volume X · Number 14

McNamee on the cover of *Time* dated October 3, 1927.
Photo provided by Time Life Pictures/Getty Images

Radio standard-setter Ted Husing. *Photo courtesy of the author's collection*

comes, you can't get up the same old excitement in your broadcast. Younger men must take over."

In 1941 he handled one of his last big assignments for NBC, the documented series, *Defense for America*. All 39 of the programs were done live, and Graham's locations ranged from diving submarines to falling parachutes. He delivered his impressions on one program as he dropped 500 feet in a parachute from Fort Benning.

McNamee, whose rise as an announcer paralleled the growth of the radio industry, said goodbye to the radio listeners for the last time on April 24, 1942, with his baritone voice: "This is Graham McNamee saying, 'Goodnight all and goodbye.'" The program was *Elsa Maxwell's Party Line*. He entered the hospital the next day, and less than a month later, May 9, 1942, he was dead at age 53 of a strep infection, his dream of moving to Southern California to once again see the glorious sunset at the Rose Bowl remained unrealized.

By the mid- to late 1930s, McNamee had lost his number-one status to Ted Husing and was doing more newsreel narrations than anything else. "You reach a point as you grow older," McNamee said a year before his death, "when a football game simply can't become the most important thing in the world. When that time

What McNamee was to NBC, Ted Husing was to CBS. Husing didn't invent radio sportscasting, but he elevated it to a profession. He was a 23-year-old roustabout with a great gift of gab when he landed his first job on WJZ in the mid-1920s. A few years later he was setting the standards for all succeeding sportscasters to follow. He was the first to combine vivid description with reportorial accuracy. Blessed with a great voice, Husing combined drama, accuracy, and action-packed descriptions to reach the top. Born Edward Britt Husing on November 27, 1901, in tiny Deming, New Mexico, he moved east with his family as his father eventually landed a job as steward of the Catholic Club at Columbia University. Young Ted became mascot of the Columbia sports teams and began laying the foundation of his sports knowledge.

At Commerce High in New York City he played football and baseball and became friends with Les Quailey, who later became his chief assistant on sports broadcasts and later the head of the sports division of the N.W. Ayer advertising agency. Ted didn't stay in high school long, quitting to spend two years bumming around the country, working in street carnivals, Midwestern wheat fields, and punching cows. After returning to New York, he joined the aviation division of the New York Police Department. There followed, at the urging of his new wife, a series of mundane jobs ranging from payroll clerk to silk mill laborer to furniture salesman. He was fired from every one.

Returning from Florida after an ill-attempted plan to cash in on the real estate boom, he picked up *The New York Times* at the train station in Washington, D.C. An ad caught his eye: "RADIO ANNOUNCER—Must be young, married, conscientious, social by nature, college graduate, have knowledge of the terminology of music and ability to say the right thing at the right time." Feeling he had nothing to lose, he replied to the ad and let his imagination take over. He gave himself a college degree, from Harvard no less; told of his love of opera and symphonic music, of which he knew nothing; and battled against more than 600 applicants in two weeks to get the job. In his 1935 book, *Ten Years Behind the Mike*, Husing talked about his first audition: "If they didn't actually ask to see the sheepskin, I felt I might possibly get away from the cultural part of it. Maybe I had grown up on the sidewalks of New York, but I wasn't exactly a dese-dose guy. Association with the sons of Columbia professors had given me an early

chance to hear the correct lingo, so even when riding the bumpers I spoke the King's English as well as I could and maybe better than some college men."

Over the course of a week, the 610 were trimmed to six and Husing was still in the group. The musical category was whittling down the numbers more than any other, and Ted shuttered to think what would happen when it came his turn. He then caught a break. The assistant manager of the station, a West Point grad, took a liking to him. Ted decided to come clean about his lack of musical acumen, and the man quickly helped him master different composers and their works. He passed the musical audition, barely. Next came extemporizing, which for Ted was easy. A bad air

Ted Husing. *Drawing courtesy of the author's collection*

Tracks 7–9

crash had occurred the day before, and Husing read as much as he could about it. He needed every bit of information because the station heads kept him talking for more than 35 minutes. He got the job at $45 a week and rushed out to buy a hand-me-down dinner suit, his first. Formal attire was part of the gig in those early years. It was September 13, 1924. His first assignment was to read a stock market report.

Husing's first sports assignment came in November 1925 when he assisted J. Andrew White at the Penn-Cornell football game at the new Franklin Field in Philadelphia. Ted found WJZ's perch in a monkey tower used for hoisting concrete. It was raining, and their only shelter was a tarpaulin thrown over a scaffold. As the start of the game drew near, White had still not appeared. "As the seconds ticked off, I began

Husing at Lake Placid. **Photo provided by AP/WWP**

to get nervous," Ted remembered in his book *Ten Years Before the Mike*. "Soon I got the signal to start talking on a hookup that included Washington, D.C., Boston, Pittsburgh, and Schenectady. I talked about the weather, the crowd, the bands, everything but the teams, because I didn't know anything about them. Then, just in time, the Major arrived and he broadcast the game with no aid other than his eyesight and what information I could scribble on paper for him." In return he let Ted comment on the game between quarters. Afterward he told Ted he'd use him more on football the following season. Husing learned on that rainy day in Philadelphia that there was more to radio than enunciating genteel phrases in a plush studio. Radio could be a thrilling adventure, and he was about to join the soldiers of fortune who saw history made before their eyes.

Husing (left) signs to do play-by-play for the Baltimore Colts of the All-American Football Conference in 1947. *Photo courtesy of the author's collection*

Husing broadcast his first play-by-play football game in 1926 when Princeton hosted Navy at Palmer Stadium. In order to identify players, he built a mechanical identification machine of apartment house doorbell boards. When NBC began operating in January 1927, he quit his job at WJZ and headed for Boston where he helped inaugurate the radio station of the *Boston Transcript* newspaper. Husing did it all, including the home games of the Boston Braves. He returned to New York in the fall of 1927 to broadcast the Columbia football games on station WHN. New York's first radio critic, Raymond Yates, wrote in the November 21, 1927, *Herald-Tribune*: "Probably the deficiencies of the McNamee-Carlin reports would have passed unnoticed if Mr. Edward Husing of WHN had not entered the arena of radio football with his descriptions of Columbia and other games. In this almost-ended season, Mr. Husing has consistently given more complete information, more accurate and prompt news of the changing position of the ball and more acute observations than either of the more noted announcers. Mr. Husing is likely to become radio's most appreciated football describer, unless of course, Mr. McNamee and Mr. Carlin come to realize that the primary purpose of a football broadcast is not to furnish verbal entertainment but to provide immediate news of what the 22 football players are doing."

Husing made his share of bloopers when he started, but he had a fierce desire to prove his competence. He cultivated relationships with football coaches and baseball managers, boxers and referees, trainers and jockeys.

J. Andrew White, by this time the president of the new Columbia Broadcasting System, offered Husing a job as his assistant, and he began work on Christmas Day in 1927. In 1928 he shared microphone duties for the Yankee-Cardinal World Series as well as a complete schedule of college football games. It was his first crack on a network. He also broadcast the U.S. Open tennis tournament at Forest Hills and had a harrowing experience leaning out a 20-story building broadcasting the arrival of the Graf Zeppelin. Just before 1928 ended, a wealthy young businessman named William S. Paley purchased the network and launched CBS and Ted Husing into a new era.

Husing led off 1929 by broadcasting the Army-Stanford and East-West football games, which were the first games ever broadcast on CBS. Up until the historic 1935 Ohio State-Notre Dame football classic, Husing always said the Lafayette-Penn State clash in 1929 was the top game he ever broadcast. With five seconds remaining in a fierce defensive struggle, Lafayette led 3-0. The game seemed over as the Maroons punted to the great Penn State duo of Frank Dietrich and Cooper French. As the ball was snapped, the referee blew the final whistle, but the play still had to be completed. French caught the ball on his own 40 and headed for the right sideline as the entire Lafayette team stormed down the field. Just as French was about to be tackled, he lateraled the ball to Dietrich who headed for the opposite sideline, following his blockers and scoring the game's only touchdown some 30 seconds after the final gun had sounded.

Another of his early football memories was the Notre Dame-Army game of November 30, 1930, at cold, foggy, and drizzly Soldier Field in Chicago. Knute Rockne was coaching his last Irish team before his tragic death in a 1931 airplane crash. Notre Dame was unbeaten while Army had struggled all season, but the weather evened the playing field, and with five minutes left there was still no score. "The Irish pulled their famous 'perfect play,'" recalled Husing in *Ten Years Behind the Mike*. "Taking the ball from Frank Carideo and faking an end sweep, Marchy Schwartz cut back and broke through, slogging 58 yards through the mud for a touchdown. Carideo converted, and the 7-0 score looked like the end. But it wasn't. Army received Notre Dame's kick, advanced the ball to its 32, was held there and punted. The ball was downed on Notre Dame's 17-yard line. Two minutes to go, the fog was closing in black and the crowd began to file out. On third and nine, Carideo punted, but Army end Dick King blocked it and the ball went rolling back. King dived into Carideo to prevent a recovery. Trice and

Price of Army went after the ball, which rolled across the goal line. Trice dove on it and it was an Army touchdown. Brochous failed on the point after kick, but it was a moral victory for Army and one of those near-upsets that make sport the drama it is."

Ted Husing had two special partners, Les Quailey and Jimmy Dolan, spanning a period of 17 years. Quailey worked with Ted from 1930 to 1936 before joining N.W. Ayer advertising in Philadelphia where he handled the Atlantic Refining radio sports sponsorship account, helping to launch the careers of countless sportscasters. Quailey met Husing at Commerce High School in Manhattan. Les went on to an excellent career as a quarterback at little Alfred College near Buffalo.

Quailey took the assistant's job because he felt the travel would help in his desire to become a coach. "Ted was close to coaches because he wanted to learn the game inside and out," Quailey said. "Knute Rockne did more to help Ted learn football than anybody, along with Harry Kipke at Michigan, Dick Hanley of Northwestern, Jock Sutherland at Pitt, Bernie Bierman of Minnesota, and Gar Davidson of Army." Les said getting cooperation from coaches and colleges was a lot tougher then than in modern-day sports. "Some coaches wouldn't even give us their starting lineup. Our broadcast position was usually on a roof or across the field from the press box, so if we made a mistake there was no way we could get a correction on it. The only serious mistake I remember making was during the 1930 Notre Dame-Pitt game when I had Moon Mullins scoring a touchdown for the Irish when in reality it was Joe Savoli. Fortunately a newspaperman happened to overhear us and corrected me. I, in turn,

corrected Husing, and I never heard the end of it. He didn't tolerate mistakes."

Husing was the first to bring advance preparation and thorough research into his sports broadcasting. Ted and his partners would begin planning for the next football season as soon as the current one ended. "When they trot on the field," Husing said in his book, "we know the men, their individual specialties and

Les Quailey (left) and Husing prepare for the 1933 meeting of Ohio State and Michigan. *Photo courtesy of the author's collection*

their group combinations in play almost as well as if we had coached them ourselves."

Today we take for granted the fact that players have numbers and oftentimes names on their uniforms. When Quailey started as Husing's spotter, numbers were on the back of uniforms only. Illinois was the first he remembers wearing numbers on front and back in the Illini's 1930 game with Army. "When it became required in the Big Ten, some of the coaches would make the number on the front unreadable."

Husing was a stickler for accuracy, and one of his secrets was an electric annunciator spotting board he perfected along with Quailey and engineer Jack Norton. Knute Rockne was a great admirer of the annunciator, which came about through a natural evolution of writing names on paper and pointing to them with a pencil. It developed into slanted frames made of apartment house doorbell panels with slots to house players' names and then became a light system that would illuminate the player who had the ball. The annunciator had 22 slots covered with glass on which were written the players' names. There was a white light under each of them and a separate keyboard box with 22 buttons controlling the lights. They also devised a method to pinpoint plays and formations. With Quailey working the lights by the touch system and keeping his eyes focused on the game, Ted could rely squarely on the box for information. Husing used to carry the box under a cloak and kept a mysterious air about his magic helper. "During a football broadcast we seldom speak to each other," Husing told a newspaper reporter, "and then only in monosyllables through our headphones. Often Les comes out of a broadcast with a splitting headache from eyestrain and

concentration. When we arrived at the stadium to broadcast the Army-Notre Dame game in Chicago in 1930, I had mislaid my spectacles. It was a dark, rainy, afternoon and I couldn't even see the sidelines from our perch. The players were just blurs to me. Yet, because of Quailey's work on the annunciator that day, I broadcast the game so accurately that a Chicago newspaper committee, comparing my description with the wire reports, gave me a special commendation."

The human element was still important, and on one occasion, Ted made an on-air slip that turned into a national story and forced his expulsion from the Harvard sporting scene. It happened during the 1931 Harvard-Dartmouth game. Finding fault with the play of star Harvard quarterback Barry Wood and deploring one particular play, Husing referred to Wood's play as "putrid," incensing Harvard followers. As it turned out, Wood later rallied the Crimson to a 7-6 victory. Student condemnation of Husing brought disbarment by Harvard authorities. Harvard athletic director William Bingham announced the ban: "No announcer can come into Harvard Stadium and refer to any play made by any boy on the Harvard football team or any other team as putrid. Mr. Husing will not be admitted to the stadium in the capacity of announcer for any future Harvard game." CBS reacted by issuing their own statement, calling it "a pity that the work of one of the nation's most distinguished sports announcers were to be censored and hampered to this extent because of the choice of an unfortunate word in the stress of covering a football game."

Husing himself regretted his choice of words but said he was striving to be interesting and vivid and had no idea he was going to offend anyone. "As a sports announcer I can only say that if I and my fellows are to serve the public we must not be unduly constrained by deference to either side in the contest." Husing said he probably expressed the feelings of most of the Harvard rooters present when he threw out the line, "Wood is certainly playing a putrid game today." But in sports, one minute you're a louse and the next a hero. Two plays later Wood tossed the winning touchdown pass. Husing finished the broadcast raving once more about Barry Wood, but the damage had been done. Husing waited a year before making peace with Harvard, convincing them that his slur was not premeditated in any way. He referred to Wood as one of the greatest players in the country and named Barry to his 1931 All-Radio football team.

Only on rare occasions did Husing let Les speak into the microphone. One moment occurred during the historic Notre Dame-Ohio State game of 1935. "I had written in my pregame copy that if Notre Dame had a chance, Bill Shakespeare would have to have an outstanding game," Quailey recalled. "In the first half, Shakespeare didn't do anything. Andy Pilney replaced him and ran wild. But it was Shakespeare who threw the crucial pass to Wayne Milner to pull it out for the Irish, and Ted asked me to repeat my pregame prediction. Truthfully I didn't think Notre Dame had a chance in that game. (They won 18-13.) Red Barber, covering the game for WLW in Cincinnati, said before the kickoff that he was going to treat the game as a spectacle because of the crowd, the buildup, and the tension. As things turned out, there was a little more than spectacle in that game."

Quailey's successor, Jimmy Dolan, took over in 1937 and spent 11 years with Husing before becoming an executive with CBS sports. Dolan lived directly across the street from Les on 57th Street. Jimmy Dolan remembered playing football in Central Park with Ted Husing at center, Les Quailey at quarterback, and himself at end. Jimmy said Ted had a penchant for big words and was quite proud of it, because he never graduated from high school. Dolan left a newspaper job to replace Quailey as Husing's assistant in 1936. "I was full-time producer, spotter, and statistician, wanting no part of air work because Ted was so good. He was always in control of his voice. He could bring you to the edge of your seat without screaming. He had a sense of pacing and an ability to transfer what he saw very accurately. He loved the language, the sound of it and the flow of it."

Because of their preparation, arriving on Thursday to begin scouting the teams, they made few mistakes, but like Quailey, Dolan remembers a doozie. "One year we did a Navy-Princeton game in Baltimore and blew a touchdown. Neither Ted nor I had seen the official raise his arms to signify the score. On the next play they were getting ready to kick the conversion and I nearly died. I bumped Ted right away and he turned pale. Immediately he said, 'Ladies and gentlemen, I have just missed a touchdown.' He was honest about it. On the way back on the train we were still so upset we couldn't eat."

Before a game, Ted and Jimmy both became very tense. They would sit in silence minutes before airtime, wondering in their minds if they had overlooked anything in the way of preparation. Once the broadcast began, all of the tension disappeared. "I don't think Ted was happy when he accepted the big contract to become a disc jockey," Dolan remarked. "He loved music, and he did do West Point and the Colts during that era, but I think he missed getting around to the various colleges and the other events he had covered for years. Then came his illness which none of us, including Ted, was able to diagnose for a long period. It wasn't until one Sunday football game at the Polo Grounds when an usher told me that he had seen Ted limping, that I knew something was wrong. I found out a mysterious ailment was perplexing him, and he didn't want to see people, like myself, because of it. One day I took him to the Heisman Trophy dinner, and

Jimmy Dolan (upper right) was Husing's second assistant. Dolan (middle) and Husing (right) at the U.S. Naval Academy. **Photos courtesy of CBS**

he told me something serious was wrong with him. After that, because of his pride, he didn't want to see me, even though he was only 54 years old." Eventually, doctors discovered a brain tumor and his condition progressively worsened. The *This Is Your Life* show with Ralph Edwards recounted his story with athletic greats Alice Marble, Ralph Guldahl, and Harry Kipke among those making guest appearances. Tom Harmon told Ted they were going to dinner, and when he appeared without a tie, Tom gave him one of his, coincidentally with the same initials, T.H. "Ted was delighted with the program," said Dolan. "His doctors said it did more for him mentally than any amount of therapy in a hospital. It convinced him he was not forgotten. Even though he was in a wheelchair, he still carried himself in a professional manner, and when his eyes saw the microphone, he reacted as I thought he would, a pro's pro."

Husing didn't only excel in football, but was a master at tennis, track, golf, and the Olympic Games in Berlin in 1936. Armed with a huge ego and the talent to match it, Husing vaulted to the top of his profession in the 1930s. Conciseness was Ted's motto. His streamlined speech was crisp and to the point. He never got ruffled and had an unlimited vocabulary. In talking about a football defense, for instance, he referred to the secondary and then the tertiary.

A year later, in 1937, Husing told a reporter, "The day of the Ted Husings and Graham McNamees in football broadcasting is near an end. We're the last of our clan, for the network broadcasting of games is rapidly on the wane. Local stations are taking over the broadcasts in their territories and instead of one or two key voices airing the big games this fall, you are going to find nearly a hundred breathless commentators in the football radio boxes."

After 19 years as radio's highest paid announcer, Husing left CBS in 1946 to become radio's highest paid disc jockey. *Ted Husing's Bandstand* on WMGM paid him a yearly salary of $250,000, an astronomical sum in postwar America. He still kept a hand in sportscasting, broadcasting the fortunes of the Baltimore Colts in their inaugural 1947 season in the All-America Football Conference.

Many did not like Husing. He had a huge ego and a biting tongue. He liked the high life, associating with society types and famous people. He was an inveterate gambler and threw his money away as fast as anyone. He was especially adept at verbally knocking his competitors.

A series of operations for a brain tumor in 1954 cost Husing his sight and, temporarily, his speech. He was just 55 years old when doctors told him his condition was terminal. He wrote another book, *My Eyes Are in My Heart*, which dealt with his many physical troubles. By the fall of 1957, he felt he was well enough to resume broadcasting as he had regained some of his sight. He even signed a contract with CBS in August 1957, but by the following February CBS announced his contract was not being renewed because of diminishing voice quality brought on by his illness. He moved west to California to live with his mother. Near the end, paralyzed and blind, Husing commented on his fate in his book. "This operation took my sight and my hearing and my voice for a while. And I had to use a cane even with my mother—an octogenarian—leading me around. There isn't much left. I can remember when I was climbing up the steps of stadia carrying 60 pounds of equipment. Now I can't do a darn thing." Former Michigan star Tom Harmon, by then an L.A. sportscaster, befriended Husing in his last years, prompting Ted to say, "Tom lifted me out of obscurity and brought me back." Ted Husing died on August 10, 1962, at age 60. It's safe to say, no broadcaster before or since combined the reportorial ability, accuracy, word pictures, vocabulary, voice, and dramatic inflection into one package. New York columnist Whitney Bolton wrote after Husing's death:

Husing after brain surgery in 1957. *Photo courtesy of the author's collection*

"The art of growing up is a difficult one at best for anyone. For a youngster who struck it too rich too soon, it was impossible. But the day he learned that he couldn't see he did a lot of growing up in a great big hurry. Husing, once knocked down, looked up from the floor and faced truth. The ego died quickly when the darkness came, but the pride lived on and refused to give in. He grew up, faced his torments, reevaluated his life and became, if I may risk sounding maudlin, a man."

William Chenault Munday was the most obscure of the "Big Three" but also the most colorful. Armed with an unmistakable Southern drawl and a football vocabulary that spoke of the end zone as "the land of milk and honey," and "Beulah land," and "crapshooters formations," Munday carved a football broadcasting reputation in the South that soon brought him national fame. He called the last 12 inches between the ball and the goal line, "the most valuable piece of Georgia real estate between Rabun Gap and Tybee Light." 💿

The native Georgian attended the University of Georgia, graduating in the class of 1925. At Georgia he edited the campus newspaper, *The Red and Black*, and became the star left-handed pitcher of the baseball team. After graduation he tried his hand at pro baseball, reporting to the Salisbury club of the Piedmont League, but his wildness led him from the pitcher's mound to covering sports for *The Atlanta Journal* in 1926. After broadcasting some Atlanta Cracker baseball games for WSB, he was soon on his way to the top in radio. Lambin Kay, the pioneer announcer of WSB, asked Munday to broadcast the Southern Conference basketball tourney, and within a few hours he had become the trailblazing sports announcer of the South. In 1928, Munday received his first nationwide exposure when he was interviewed at halftime of the Yale-Georgia game in New Haven. Kay had notified NBC that Munday, covering the game for the *Journal*, might make a good halftime guest. Munday made such an impression that NBC hired him to broadcast football for the 1929 season. It also led to his crowning achievement, broadcasting the 1929 Rose Bowl with Graham McNamee on a coast-to-coast hookup. McNamee took Munday under his wing, but neither was totally prepared for what happened during that memorable Rose Bowl. The game would immortalize both Munday and University of California center Roy Riegels. Reports conflict on exactly what happened. One report said that when Riegels picked up a fumble by Georgia Tech's Stumpy Thomason, he headed in the wrong direction toward his own goal line. McNamee was so dumbfounded he stopped talking while Munday grabbed the reins and announced the fabled "wrong-way" run to the stunned nationwide audience. This was partly true in that McNamee was totally perplexed, but he wasn't broadcasting at the moment of the run. Neither was Munday. A third announcer, Carl Haverlin, described Riegels's 83-yard dash to destiny that lifted unbeaten Georgia Tech to an 8-7 win over Riegels's California Bears. Munday had just finished reporting the first quarter and had handed the mike over to Haverlin when the famous run occurred. Yet Munday became identified with the broadcast because of the way he capitalized on its popularity. "He sort of 'adopted' the situation," Munday's former friend Furman Bisher said. "I never did challenge Bill, because there was nothing to be gained by it. I heard the game as a little boy in North Carolina. There was no point in taking away that little edge of confidence that Bill had built his entire career on."

Longtime announcing legend Ernie Harwell, who grew up listening to Bill Munday, said: "Bill made all of us from the South sound like Connecticut Yankees. He was so Southern. His signature sign-on was 'How do you do, ladies and gentlemen of the loud speaker ensemble.' He had some great phrases that later influenced Red Barber and myself. When a man was tackled, he was 'brought down to terra firma.' Plus the 'land of milk and honey' and the 'crapshooters' formation. He was very colorful, very slow talking but unique in his style."

In 1951 Bill was in New York to be interviewed by Ben Grauer on NBC's 25th anniversary celebration. He breathlessly recreated, with sound effects,

Announcer Bill Munday had a unique style and delivery that connected with his listeners in the South. *Photo courtesy of the University of Georgia*

Riegels's historic boo-boo: "Stumpy Thomason back in the tail. Peter Pund snaps the ball to Thomason, who swings wide to his left. He's following good interference. He cuts back off tackle and is through for three, four, five, six, seven yards. BAM! He fumbles when hit around the ankle in the open field. There's a mad scramble for the pigskin. Center Roy Riegels of

Cal catches it on the bounce and heads for the Tech goal. He's swerving, he's fighting, he's squirming, Tech tacklers all around him. He can't get away. He pivots and—whoa! WAIT A MINUTE. WHAT IS THIS? WHY, HE'S TURNED COMPLETELY AROUND, AND HE'S HEADING FOR HIS OWN GOAL, 65 YARDS AWAY! Halfback Benny Lom pops out of nowhere and tries to stop him, but he can't. He can't. He's hollering and hollering! But Riegels doesn't hear him. Now everybody is after him, both teams helter-skelter all over the field. Everybody is going crazy! Riegels crosses the 10, and Lom grabs him by the arm. They're at the three, and Lom is turning him around. He's hit by the entire Georgia Tech team!" Cal was given the ball on their own one-yard line. Riegels, left in the game, centered the ball to Lom who punted from his end zone but Vance Maree blocked the kick. The ball was last touched by Cal halfback Stan Barr before it rolled out of bounds for a safety. Riegels outplayed Tech's All-America center Peter Pund in the second half, but the damage was done as Cal lost 8-7. During the game, when the Yellow Jackets employed an unusual formation that had the center and the quarterback back to back, Munday called it "the crapshooters formation," because it reminded him of boys shooting dice.

This one game propelled Munday to sportscasting heights. During the 1929 season he was at the mike for Georgia's historic Sanford Stadium dedication victory over Yale. He also did the Georgia-Oglethorpe game in Sanford Stadium that year, describing the runs of Oglethorpe halfback Luke Appling, a future baseball Hall of Famer.

In 1930 he announced the Notre Dame-USC game on NBC for the national championship, won by the Irish 27-0, in what turned out to be Knute Rockne's final game as coach. Also in 1930 he announced the Yale-Harvard game, the first football broadcast to be short-waved overseas. "In the old days we used those massive, monstrous mikes that you could talk into but

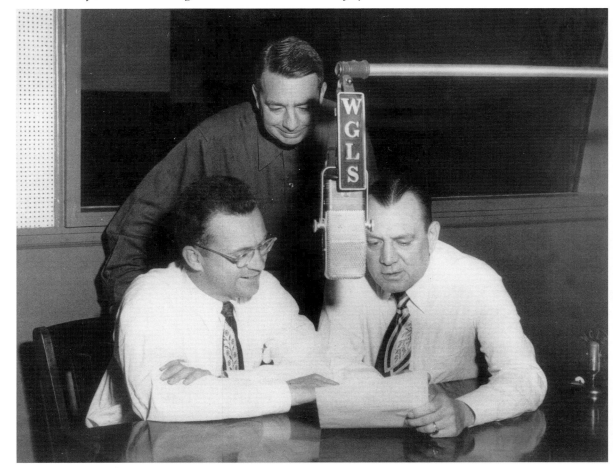

Ernie Harwell (left) and Munday (right) partner up behind the mike under the watchful eye of station manager Sam Kane. *Photo courtesy of the author's collection*

had to peer around to see what was happening on the field," said Munday to reporter Furman Bisher. "Whenever you decided to give the radio audience a bit of color in the way of the roar of the crowd or the bands, you had to swing those bulky instruments plumb around so they faced the playing field. On one occasion when I had an assignment to broadcast a Big Ten game in the Midwest for NBC, I was placed in a booth that would accommodate only me and a lone spotter. My engineer was forced to stand outside in sub-zero cold and nearly froze to death. Once, when Nebraska came east to play Pittsburgh, I used a Negro Pullman porter as my spotter. The reason this fellow knew the players was because Nebraska traveled on the train he was portering."

Respected New York writer and chronicler of sports' golden age Paul Gallico paid Munday a compliment in the July 29, 1929, edition of the *New York Daily News:* "Suddenly from the loudspeaker comes a fresh new voice, a voice that for all its Southern cadences and rhythmics is letting fly a bristling, rapid fire of description, couched in a new and gay phraseology, teeming with good humor and enthusiasm, and demonstrating without ostentation how sports on radio should be spoken."

In 1936, CBS hired Munday to do the play by play on its Orange Bowl broadcast. It was the Bowl's second year but first to be broadcast on radio. Munday described a thriller as Catholic University, then a power, held off Mississippi 20-19.

Munday was the first of a long line of Southern broadcasters who reached the heights: Mel Allen, Red Barber, Lindsey Nelson, Ernie Harwell, Keith Jackson, Russ Hodges, Jimmy Dudley, and Arch McDonald.

Harwell worked with Munday on WSB in Atlanta. "I know I copied his style," Ernie admitted, "and I felt that Red Barber had a very similar style to Munday's. It was a down-to-earth, Southern homespun type of delivery with expressions that come from the kitchen table and the backyard."

"The most amazing thing about Bill was his memory," said longtime Georgia network partner Ed Thilenius. "He could remember the big plays, the score, even the weather on a game played 25 years ago. Bill was truly an amazing fellow and a wonderful one."

The man whom journalist O.B. Keeler referred to as "the vocal eye," and whom *New York Telegram* radio editor Jack Foster dubbed, "The Georgia Drawl," announced all of the Georgia games in 1935, Alabama in 1936, and LSU in 1937. Life was thrilling and the current was swift for Munday, and by the late 1930s he had drifted into radio and personal oblivion. Alcohol was his downfall. "McNamee and I would work games together," Munday once told Furman Bisher, "and every time we'd get back to the hotel there would be a bottle of booze. First it was a nip or two, and then it was a slug or two. I began to notice that I was doing all the drinking and McNamee was just watching. I soon found out that I had a low capacity, but that didn't cut down my appetite for the stuff." There were rumors that some of his rival announcers, knowing his weakness for alcohol, enhanced his drinking by encouraging and prodding him into consuming more. The result was he lost his network job, came back to *The Atlanta Journal* and lost that job, too. He wandered the streets begging money from friends to buy a drink. "That's when I met him," Harwell recalled. "He was walking the streets, begging for quarters and dimes."

He moved from job to job, even working as the P.A. announcer for Cracker games at Ponce de Leon Park. Again he didn't last long.

Over 10 years and numerous comebacks went by before he hit bottom in early 1949. He then found the Lord and never took another drink. In 1951 he joined Harwell and several other broadcasters on Red Barber's *CBS Football Roundup*. He stayed on the *Roundup* for five years and then joined Thilenius on the broadcasts of Georgia football. He was the regular announcer for the Gator Bowl for many years. Furman Bisher became his closest friend in Atlanta, and he maintained his friendship with Harwell, often visiting the then-Oriole announcer in Baltimore and New York

Munday (left) was known for his down-home style and later became the University of Georgia's goodwill ambassador. *Photo courtesy of the University of Georgia*

City. "I always enjoyed being with Bill. He was a great friend and could have been one of the top network announcers if booze hadn't done him in, but God bless him, he later reformed, joined Alcoholics Anonymous, and became a member of society again."

Munday became the University of Georgia's greatest goodwill ambassador. His favorite Bulldog team was the last one he covered, the 1964 Bulldogs, "because they were successful when everybody picked them to be at the bottom of the pack." The last game he witnessed saw the Bulldogs stage a great comeback to beat Florida in Jacksonville. A few days later he suffered a heart attack. In recovery, he told a reporter, "I am a Bulldog born, a Bulldog bred, and when I die, I'll be a Bulldog dead."

Bill Munday died on February 26, 1965, "prancing into Beulah land," as one friend put it. Atlanta columnist John Martin wrote the following day: "The most famous old Bulldog lefthander walked off the mound to the dugout yesterday. Today he rests in the red clay he religiously worshipped and eulogized. From obscurity he rocketed into the stratosphere, then tobogganed on a cork to the hinges of hell. Before the old Bulldog's heart bounced the wrong way, his recovery outweighed all his fumbles. No, he had no enemies. Nobody except John Barleycorn, the 100-proof slugger who knocked Munday out of his regular turn as the ace of the 'Big three.' So this fall, when his cherished Bulldogs kick off, Bill Munday won't be there to say 'He was brought to Mother Earth from whence he sprang.' Instead he'll be a saintly spectator, watching silently from the 50-yard line, and his spirit and heart will be in Sanford Field. He'll be hoping it's a good day, 'ladies and gentlemen.'"

Artwork courtesy of Robert T. Handville

More Pigskin Pioneers

The Golden Age of Sports in the 1920s led to the Golden Age of Radio. In the two decades that followed radio's introduction to sports, football's popularity reached the heights. By this time, in the late 1920s, the game had spread its Eastern roots to the gridirons of the Midwest and the up-and-coming powers of the West Coast. Down South, Alabama, Georgia, and Tennessee were powers, and the Texas Longhorns were serving notice in the Southwest. Just about every school of importance was airing its games on radio.

Not so in the professional leagues. It wasn't until the late 1930s that the NFL began making a name for itself, and not a very big name at that.

But radio, and later television, would endear football to the hearts of sports fans around the country, and the men behind the mike would set the scenes that would be immortalized in the nation's memory.

But it wasn't easy and glamorous in the beginning. Early-day obstacles were massive, especially in the sport of football. No booths, bulky equipment, dealing with the elements, slipshod numbering systems and no background information all tested the mettle of the early trailblazers. In many cases games were recreated from a studio with crowd noise and sound effects added. Others braved the elements and went to the scene, climbing up ladders to rooftop perches or oftentimes sitting in the stands amidst the fans.

Unlike television, which lessened the importance of the broadcaster since the viewers were watching what he was watching, radio provided the canvas for the broadcaster to paint. He had to combine knowledge of sports with the voice and excitement and expertise to impart word pictures that the public could

A press box in 1946. *Photo provided by Mark Kauffman/Time Life Pictures/Getty Images*

follow. These were the golden voices of the golden age of broadcasting. They brought us the roar of the crowd, the marching bands and the "tumult and the shouting," as Grantland Rice so aptly put it.

The pioneers of football broadcasting were early wordsmiths who brought the thrills of the gridiron to America's living rooms and automobiles. Long before instant replay, rights fees, *SportsCenter*, slo-mo, and computer simulators, these icons were defining Saturday afternoons in the fall and bringing us the exciting exploits of the NFL on Sunday.

The legendary Fielding Yost coached the Wolverines and gave permission to broadcast the game on a "one time only," experimental basis because the seats had been sold out for weeks in advance. "It sure was a sellout," Ty said later. "Doc and I had to pay to get in just like everyone else." Yost had expressed fear that the broadcast would hurt ticket sales, but before the next home game, Ty's broadcast had helped swamp the ticket office with requests. A delighted Yost happily arranged for more broadcasts. Michigan was enjoying great gridiron success in those years, and radio only

In the state of Michigan, there was only one broadcasting name that mattered: Edwin Lloyd "Ty" Tyson. It was back in 1924 when Tyson, then in his third year at WWJ in Detroit, broadcast the first football game ever in Detroit and one of the first college football games ever aired in the Midwest. The site was old Ferry Field in Ann Arbor. It was a crisp afternoon on October 25, 1924, when the slim, dapper broadcaster with a waggish eye and an air of confidence propped himself behind a carbon mike as big as his 1924 fedora in the fifth row of the stands in the east end zone and described Michigan's 13-6 win over Wisconsin. He was helped by color man Leonard "Doc" Holland.

Ty Tyson (right) and Leonard Holland cover the Wolverines from the press box in Ann Arbor. *Photo provided by Bentley Historical Library, University of Michigan*

enhanced it. Ty's descriptions of legendary Wolverine Benny Oosterbaan's heroics in the mid-1920s helped sell thousands of radios in the state of Michigan.

"The players wore no numbers," Ty remembered in a 1967 interview at his Grosse Pointe, Michigan, home. "We had our work cut out for us. Since we worked out in the open, with fans all around us, we had to fight to keep the shouts and screams off the air. Some of them weren't in very clean taste. Prohibition was in effect, but liquor bottles were everywhere. There was no shelter. It was wide-open broadcasting on a wide-open, windy day with a wide-open microphone. In those early years we sat huddled together through drenching rains and blanketing snowstorms. Back in those early years there were only 16 or 18 players to remember. Now it's an era for specialists. I remember the first out-of-town football game WWJ brought to Detroit radio fans. It was from Ohio State in 1926, and the telephone line charges were almost $2,200, a huge sum of money. Those were the days when we had to tap the mike each time we used it to shake up the carbon so it would work."

Ty Tyson was born on May 11, 1888, in a small Pennsylvania town called Phillipsburg, located in the central part of the state. At an early age his family

Holland and Tyson would cover Michigan games on WWJ for 27 years.
Photo provided by Bentley Historical Library, University of Michigan

moved to nearby Tyrone where, legend has it, he got his nickname. He thought he would follow his father in the wallpaper and stationery business after spending a year at Penn State where he played freshman football. He played semi-professional football in the coal-mining area where the pro game was born and nurtured. Ty and his boyhood buddies, Fred Waring and Bill Holliday, were big fans of vaudeville and silent movies and often put on their own minstrel shows. Waring, along with his brother, Tom, and his friends, Poley McClintock and Fred Buck, formed their own orchestra, which later became Fred Waring and the Pennsylvanians.

World War I changed Ty's life drastically as he spent 22 months overseas in the 103 Trench Mortar Battery where he fought in some of the bloodiest battles of the war. He returned to the paper mill business after the war, but things weren't the same because his friend Holliday had moved to Detroit to work for an adding machine company.

When radio debuted in the early 1920s, Holliday was fascinated and became WWJ's first program manager as well as on-air entertainer. He booked Waring's band for a gig at the station and at the Madison Theater in Detroit. Waring mentioned to Holliday that he should hire Ty, and in 1922 Ty, tossing an extra shirt and a pair of socks into his suitcase, headed west to begin his radio career. He booked the acts, played the records, and read the news. He introduced Charles Lindbergh to Detroit audiences as well as President Herbert Hoover, Babe Ruth, Will Rogers, Ty Cobb, and Knute Rockne.

Ty began broadcasting Tiger games in 1927 from the upper deck of Navin Field. His penchant for accuracy, his dry humor, and his understanding of the game made him a universal favorite. "I stuck to the game and didn't care about color," he said, proudly. "Others like Graham McNamee talked a great scene, but they didn't know much about sports. I didn't think it was necessary to keep talking all the time."

By 1931 Ty was a long established fixture as the voice of the Wolverines. "High up in the handle of the huge cup, which is the University of Michigan Stadium in Ann Arbor, high above the waves of bounding, leaping color and rolling sound, sit two men each football day, who have become the eyes of thousands. Up there in their little coop, Ty Tyson and Doc Holland

toast their shins against an electric heater while the human icicles out on the concrete benches grow stiffer and stiffer with each sweep of the north wind," wrote Herschell Hart in a 1931 *Detroit News* story.

He always considered football the tougher sport than baseball to broadcast. "Baseball's a cinch," Ty said. "The players are generally in set positions. There is no deception to baseball." Ty worked the games for years with WWJ announcer Holland. They developed a system of signals whereby Doc would alert Ty of any feature that may have slipped past him, the yardage gained, and the name of the runner or the tackler. There were times when it took two sets of eyes to be sure of what the mud-splattered number really was. "Not a word is spoken except what you hear on the air," Hart wrote in his 1931 article. "A pencil points to a series of numbers, not necessarily those corresponding to the players, but numbers which have a significance pertaining to the play. A hand waves, a finger points and a head shakes. They may be warmer, but think of having to watch a game and not be able to yell—at least once."

Fan Elmer J. Grank wrote in the *Detroit News*: "Anybody who is not quite familiar with the game of football would not understand it as well at the game as they would right at home listening to Ty Tyson describe it. Here's hoping that Mr. Tyson lives forever in the hearts of radio fans."

In 1947 Ty was honored for his 25 years in radio at WWJ. Mayor Edward J. Jeffries proclaimed a day in his honor, and a huge banquet was held. "This radio must be here to stay," said Ty in his closing remarks. "I think I can send to Tyrone for my other suit." He covered the Wolverines through the 1950 season. Holland

Above: Tyson (circled) at the 1924 Michigan-Wisconsin game that started it all. Right: Tyson before he retired from the mike in 1953. *Background photo provided by Bentley Historical Library, University of Michigan; foreground photo courtesy of WWJ*

served as spotter-commentator for 27 years with Ty and stayed on at WWJ through the 1970 season, a span of 46 years.

On February 27, 1953, the "Tyrone Tradition" formally retired from broadcasting and WWJ after 31 years. The retirement ceremony was broadcast live on radio and television. Old friends and coworkers were on hand while taped messages came from famous people across the country who were touched by Ty over the years. A gold-plated carbon mike of the type he used when he first began in radio was presented to Ty. On the mike were inscribed the dates of Ty's firsts—from the Gold Cup boat races to the first televised game from Briggs Stadium.

"No man anywhere endeared himself so much to his listening public," NBC Vice President Harry Bannister said. His friend at the *Detroit News*, George Stark, phrased it eloquently when he wrote: "You have to say that the world's first sportscaster has done his stint at last and folded up his scoring sheets. His statistical firsts are vital, but they somehow fail us, because they neglect to reproduce the booming, friendly voice with its passion for accuracy, its quick recognition of color; the voice that brought the whole wide exciting field of competitive sports into the home and made the broadcaster's name a household word and dearly loved."

Ty was 65 when he formally retired, but he assisted Bob Reynolds of WJR on Michigan State football broadcasts for several seasons thereafter. He loved to talk about the Michigan teams of the late 1930s that featured Tom Harmon and Forrest Evashevski, and the 1947 team under Fritz Crisler, which he considers the best ever. Fullback Jack Weisenburger and halfback "Bump" Elliott each averaged more than six yards a carry, while halfback Bob Chappuis was a unanimous All-America choice. "That team proved its superiority," Ty said, "by routing USC in the Rose Bowl, 49-0. Even Amos Alonzo Stagg said that Fritz's team displayed the most beautiful offensive football he had ever seen. Its artistry was almost perfect." In 1965 Ernie Harwell had him sit in on a Tiger Father's Day broadcast. It was such a hit that Ty would return often. At 77 he still had the touch.

At 7:45 a.m. on a cold Thursday morning, December 12, 1968, Ty Tyson died at age 80, and an era born in carbon microphones, tickertape baseball recreations, and crystal receivers died with him.

Ty Tyson was the first in a long line of great Michigan football announcers. Van Patrick, Bill Fleming, Bob Ufer, and Tom Hemingway were some of the others. A 1949 grad of Michigan, Fleming got his start at WUOM in 1949 for a salary of $25 a week. He joined the staff of WWJ in Detroit in 1953 and broadcast Wolverine games through 1959 when he joined ABC on their college football package. He also became a key component of ABC's *Wide World of Sports*.

Bill Fleming took over the Wolverine broadcasts from 1953 through 1959, when he joined ABC's college football team. *Photo provided by Bentley Historical Library, University of Michigan*

Van Patrick televised baseball in Cleveland and Detroit but became a fixture in the Detroit area with his broadcasts of Michigan and Detroit Lion football. Van was as much a part of Thanksgiving Day as the dressing and pumpkin pie as he hosted the national telecast of the Lions and Packers from Briggs Stadium. Bobby Layne, Joe Schmidt, Yale Lary, and Dick "Night Train" Layne became legendary players with Van at the mike. Later, he became sports director of the Mutual Radio network and broadcast Notre Dame football for seven seasons. A veteran of 39 years in broadcasting, Van Patrick died on September 29, 1974, at age 58.

What Ty Tyson was to Detroit, France Laux was to St. Louis. Starting with his spur-of-the-moment recreation of the 1927 World Series on station KVOO in Tulsa, Laux carved out a legendary career in the Midwest, mostly with the powerful KMOX in St. Louis. Although primarily known in St. Louis for his baseball work, Laux was one of the first to broadcast football, in Tulsa, in the fall of 1928. "I had been coaching high school football, and since our games were over on Friday afternoon, I was able to drive to Tulsa University, the University of Oklahoma, or the Oklahoma Aggies, which later became Oklahoma State," France said.

Born in Guthrie, Oklahoma, on December 3, 1897, James Francis "France" Laux grew up in Bristow, Oklahoma, where he garnered 16 letters in five sports, four of them in football. His great love, though, was

Van Patrick was the voice of Detroit Lions football. *Photo courtesy of the Detroit Lions*

baseball, and he dreamed of becoming a professional baseball player. "I soon found out I couldn't hit enough, and the only baseball I played after high school was semi-pro ball," France lamented in an interview.

France entered World War I with some of his high school teammates and flew in the Air Force Signal Corps over France and England. At war's end he returned to Bristow and opened a cleaning and pressing shop. Then came a real estate and insurance business, with a year spent playing college football at Oklahoma City College. On his very first play on a

Track 63; Track 5

Patrick's coverage of football on WJR made him a popular figure in the Detroit area. *Ad courtesy of News/Talk 760 WJR; photo courtesy of the Detroit Lions*

second-half kickoff, he broke in the clear only to be blindsided. He suffered a dislocated cheekbone and a broken hand. Undeterred, France played the entire season, breaking two ribs in the fourth game, necessitating a protective harness. "When George Halas formed the Decatur Staleys in 1919, the forerunner of the Chicago Bears, Charley Pickett, an old teammate from Bristow and I were offered professional contracts, but we turned them down because of the injury factor, " said France. "In those days equipment was primitive with flimsy headgear and little padding."

France Laux (above) became popular in the St. Louis area as a baseball man for KMOX, but he got his broadcasting start at KVOO in Tulsa covering football in 1927 with partner George Goodale (lower, left). *Background photo courtesy of KMOX Radio; foreground photo courtesy of KVOO*

Laux went to KMOX in 1929 and got a 30-day trial, he stayed with the station for 40 years. ***Photo courtesy of KMOX Radio***

The first football game France ever broadcast was over at Enid, Oklahoma, in 1927 with Phillips University playing Oklahoma Baptist. "We drove our Model-T right onto the sidelines and parked it about 10 yards from the field, right on the 50-yard line," France recalled. "The car was our broadcast booth. I sat in the front seat holding a microphone in one hand, juggling papers in the other, and trying to report the action all at the same time. The engineer sat in the rumble seat. We soon learned that a Model-T was fine for transportation but was no place to broadcast a football game. So the next week we went to Tahlequah,

Oklahoma, to broadcast the Northeastern Teachers-Central College game out of Edmond, and this time we came prepared. We brought along an orange crate and folding chairs. We sat the crate about six yards from the sidelines and perched the microphone right on top of it." France placed his lineup sheets and other material on the crate and after a few minutes of the broadcast felt it was smooth sailing. He forgot one important detail, however. "The flying tackle was still very much a part of college football in those days," France remembered. "A safety fielded a punt, and as he was running in front of our makeshift booth, two tacklers dove for the ball carrier with all three landing on the orange crate, sending me, my engineer, my notes, and the equipment in ten different directions. The result was we were off the air for 45 minutes trying to hurriedly reassemble the scattered mess. That was my baptism into football announcing."

France's color man on those early broadcasts was George Goodale, who would later join Gene Autry as his press agent and serve as public relations director of the Los Angeles Angels baseball team. Then he was a sportswriter for the *Tulsa World* newspaper. France Laux was the first to introduce Gene Autry to a radio audience. It was at KVOO, and at the time Gene was a telegraph operator for the Frisco railroad in Chelsea, Oklahoma. Will Rogers had heard Autry sing and told him to give radio a try. When he did, singing for free, Laux did the introduction.

France contacted KMOX in St. Louis early in 1929 asking for an announcing job. They gave him a 30-day trial, and he was still there 40 years later. The first football game he announced in St. Louis was between St. Louis University and Washington University. He

Laux prepares for a broadcast in 1934. *Photo courtesy of the author's collection*

State game. One Wisconsin-Notre Dame game stands out. "Before the game I sent my color commentator, Maurice Clifford, down to get the phonetic spelling of the players' [names] on both teams. Notre Dame was loaded with Polish boys with long names. Notre Dame ran all over Wisconsin that day, and it seemed that every substitute that entered the game was harder to pronounce than the man he replaced. Finally, Notre Dame began putting fourth stringers in, and I all but gave up. The only fourth stringer that didn't get into the game was named Smith."

France Laux stayed active as a freelance broadcaster for KMOX and other St. Louis stations until his death on November 16, 1978, at age 81.

had to stand up on the top row of the north stands at Francis Field with snow coming down. The press box was on the other side of the field, but it was so small that there wasn't any room for the radio announcer and his equipment. Conditions weren't much better at Sportsman's Park, the home of the Cardinals and Browns. He broadcast in the early days behind home plate and then the upper deck. France began broadcasting the fortunes of both St. Louis teams in 1929 and lasted 26 years, announcing nine World Series in the process.

KMOX divided its football schedule between Missouri, Illinois, Notre Dame, and Northwestern. France always made sure that they lined up Missouri's games with Oklahoma, Nebraska, and Kansas, plus the Illinois-Northwestern game and Notre Dame-Michigan

The Ohio State Buckeyes have enjoyed a proud and lengthy football tradition, both on the field and in the broadcast booth. Over the years, such recognizable names as Jack Buck, Red Barber ⊙, Ken Coleman, Bert Charles, Marv Homan, Bill McColgan, Jimmy Dudley, Jimmy Crum, Bob Neal, Rick Rizz, Terry Smith, Paul Keels, Tom Hamlin, and Tom Manning broadcast Ohio State football. For several years, before anybody thought of charging for the privilege, any station that had the gumption and the remote apparatus necessary, could find a spot somewhere at Ohio Stadium and broadcast the games. It was first come, first serve. In 1948, NBC's Bill Stern requested a booth on the Wednesday before the Ohio State-Michigan game after all of the booths were assigned. Ted Husing and CBS had gotten theirs. Stern was furious, and the best that

Top: Laux (second from right) with other reporters in 1944. Right: Laux (far left) with Harry Wismer, Harry Nash, and Craig Wood. *Photos courtesy of the author's collection*

Sports Information Director Wilbur Snypp could do was to put Stern on a temporary open-air platform overlooking the south end zone. If anything, it taught Stern that not every school would move mountains to accommodate him.

Of the aforementioned broadcasters, no one broadcast the Buckeyes longer or with more passion than Cleveland's Tom Manning. Over the years he became known as their unofficial coach, their 12th man, and the team's extra quarterback. The "Old Redhead" broadcast Ohio State football for 29 seasons.

From barking out baseball lineups through a huge megaphone at League Park in the early 1920s to the heights as a network announcer on NBC, Manning spanned the golden era of radio and sports from the rollicking 1920s to the turbulent 1960s in a career that spanned more than 40 years. Whether the assignment was World Series, Olympic games, political conventions, or air races, it did not matter. If it was important, Manning was there to broadcast it. His salary for doing a World Series game on NBC was $100 a game. If the series went four games, he got $400. If it went all seven games, which he hoped for, he received $700.

His first big Ohio State assignments were on the NBC Blue Network. NBC created two separate networks, the Red and Blue. The Red was more prestigious and commanded the biggest advertising dollars, while the Blue was the little brother of the two, airing more public service announcements so the Red could reap more advertising dollars. Legendary NBC Program Director John F. Royal, who left Cleveland for NBC and brought Manning with him, often said the Blue network saved NBC's life.

Ohio State Buckeye announcers included Jimmy Dudley (above) and the great Red Barber (right). *Background photo courtesy of WERE-AM; foreground photo courtesy of CBS*

Track 4

"On the same Saturday afternoon, Graham McNamee would announce the Army-Navy game while Ford Bond and I would be sent to Notre Dame or Ohio State," remembered Manning in a 1967 interview. In Cleveland, the Red network was on the powerful WTAM while the Blue was on WGAR. Eventually the

In the 1920s Manning began his career, which continued into the 1960s. *Photos courtesy of WTAM*

FCC broke up the Red-Blue NBC domination and the Blue network eventually became ABC.

Manning worked for several years with the legendary Graham McNamee during a time when "a newspaperman wouldn't walk on the same side of the street with a broadcasting personality. "Jealousy abounded," said Manning and McNamee became the whipping boy of the writers. "He had a brilliant voice, fluent delivery and had great enthusiasm. He was the pioneer and had to take it on the chin from all the petty critics. Graham knew his

Manning (far left) toward the end of his career, and Manning (right) with Cleveland friend Bob Hope (left) circa 1952. *Background photo courtesy of the author's collection; foreground photo courtesy of WTAM*

sports," Manning continued, "but in those days one mistake became a critic's headline."

In 1931 Manning abandoned his game-of-the-week travel doing college football on NBC and, enticed by a handsome contract from the Standard Oil Company, joined the Ohio State Buckeyes as their main play-by-play voice. For 29 consecutive seasons, Tom lived and died with the Buckeyes. "When I joined them in 1931, Ohio State was averaging about 30,000 fans a game in the giant horseshoe. When I retired in 1960 they were averaging over 80,000 a game," Tom said. "I was part

of this mania. Hundreds of games and thousands of athletes passed through my microphone into radio sets everywhere in the years I reported Ohio State football." It was many a Saturday afternoon that football fans throughout the Midwest turned on their radios and heard the "Old Redhead" shouting the laurels of Ohio State football:

"A very pleasant good afternoon football fans…From our lofty perch high on the western rim of the Ohio Stadium here at the crossroads of American football…Tom Manning speaking for NBC and inviting you to be WTAM's guest for the next three hours as we broadcast the game between the Buckeyes from Columbus and the Wolverines of Michigan..and the impact should be terrific."

In Tom's fourth season at the OSU microphone, he witnessed the greatest football game he ever saw. It was November 2, 1935, and the unbeaten Fighting Irish of Notre Dame came to Columbus to play the unbeaten Buckeyes in the first ever meeting between the two national powers. "Elmer Layden's Irish had polished off Kansas, Carnegie Tech, Wisconsin, Pitt, and Navy while Ohio State had allowed an average of just one touchdown a game in trouncing Kentucky, Drake, Northwestern, and Indiana," Manning recalled. The Drake final score had been a resounding 85-7. More than 81,000 squeezed into Ohio Stadium. The Buckeyes led 13-0 in the fourth quarter with just a few minutes left in the game. But when Ohio State was leading 13-12, the complexion changed. "Buckeye coach Francis Schmidt was so confident of victory, he began taking his regulars out, which later proved his downfall," Tom said. "He yanked his entire backfield in the fourth quarter, and according to the rule book, which stated that a player taken out in any quarter couldn't return in the same quarter, had to keep them out. Meanwhile, Notre Dame's Andy Pilney had been injured and carried off the field on a stretcher, replaced by reserve halfback Bill Shakespeare. With 32 seconds left on the clock Wayne

Manning commanded the mike for NBC. He interviewed many celebrities of the day, including Joe "E" Brown (foreground, left), Tom Mix, Tris Speaker, and Lou Boudreau. *Photos courtesy of NBC*

TOM MANNING
ALL-AMERICAN
SPORTCASTER
Daily except Sunday
6:00 to 6:10 P.M.
WTAM — Cleveland

Photos courtesy of WTAM

BIGGEST THRILL...TOM MANNING, the dean of America's sports-casters, claims that last Wednesday night's assignment as Toastmaster at FISHER FOODS 50th Anniversary celebration at the Statler was his greatest thrill. In Manning's case this really covers a lot of ground. Tom was the first World Series announcer along with GRAHAM MC-NAMEE, has broadcast championship fights from coast to coast, been on hand for Ohio State's greatest years, and was honored himself last June in a Testomonial Dinner in the Grand Ballroom of the Statler. Tom will be leaving for his annual Florida vacation in mid-February and will not return until late March. He will pick up the Indians in Milwaukee on April 12th...MILT KOMITO, formerly of WAKR-TV in Akron, and now Station Manager of WTAP-TV in Parkersburg, West Virginia was the subject of a recent article in the West Virginia edition of T V GUIDE...EMERY WESTFALL, who handles Promotion and Special Events for HIGBEE'S, has resigned to take a position in the Public Relations Department of the Ohio Bell. Resignation is effective on February 18th...

Millner sneaked a yard deep in the end zone, and while down on both knees gathered in a desperation 19-yard heave from Shakespeare for an 18-13 Notre Dame victory." Tom was so vociferous in his rooting for Ohio State that newsstand windows posted the score as "Notre Dame 18, Tom Manning 13." Added Tom, "I always said Shakespeare had a pair of rosary beads and a bottle of holy water in his back pocket."

In a footnote to that classic game, Red Barber, then the voice of the Cincinnati Reds, was also broadcasting the action, and when Millner caught the winning touchdown pass, Red's excited Notre Dame spotter ran from the booth to join the on-field celebration. Since the Irish wore numbers only on the back of their uniforms, it took Red several minutes before identifying number 38, Wayne Millner, as the player who caught the winning touchdown.

Out in Iowa City, Iowa, on that same day, Ronald Reagan was broadcasting the Iowa-Indiana game. Because of the interest in Ohio State-Notre Dame, Reagan was providing Western Union updates on the game throughout his broadcast. Knowing that Ohio State was leading 13-0 in the fourth quarter, Reagan thought the final of 18-13 Irish was a mistake, disbelieving that Notre Dame could score three touchdowns that quickly, so he never announced the final score, fearing it was a misprint.

That thrilling loss to Notre Dame was Manning's top football thrill, but one memory for its pure craziness happened on November 8, 1947, against Northwestern: "Can you imagine a game having four extra plays which resulted in a victory after the final gun had sounded?"

"The Buckeyes were in the midst of a terrible season, one which produced just two victories all year," Manning recalled. "The Wildcats scored early in the fourth quarter, and Ohio State mounted a drive that appeared to end on the one when the Buckeyes tried a fourth-down running play. With 1:47 left, many of the 70,000 plus fans headed for the exits, but after a Northwestern punt, the Buckeyes got the ball again and with 13 seconds left, a pass play put the Buckeyes on Northwestern's 12-yard line. Pandel Savic's next pass was intercepted as time expired. Northwestern appeared the winner, and the Buckeye band came out on the field. But wait! Northwestern had 12 men on the field, and Ohio State would get another shot. The Buckeyes tried a reverse, but Rodney Swinehart was tackled at the two. But the Wildcats were offsides, and the Buckeyes would get yet another play. This time Savic hit Jimmy Clark in the end zone to tie it at 6-6. The try for the point after was blocked, but again the Wildcats were offsides. This time the extra point was good, and Ohio State emerged victorious, 7-6."

Another Manning memory occurred in the 1943 season, Paul Brown's last as Buckeye coach. National champs the year before, Uncle Sam had depleted Brown's team as they exchanged their scarlet and gray colors for the olive drab of the military. Ohio State finished 3-6 in 1943, Brown's worst season in coaching. Illinois came to Columbus for the season's last home game on November 13, and it turned into a classic. When Ohio State misfired on a last-second pass into the end zone, the final gun sounded and it ended in a 26-26 tie. "I quickly recapped the action and paused for a commercial," Tom remembered. "The teams left the field and the stands emptied, and all seemed content with the outcome, except for Buckeye assistant Ernie Godfrey, who, alert as always, had noticed head linesman Paul Goebel drop a handkerchief to signify a penalty, but on hearing the gun sound had quickly stuffed it in his back pocket hoping no one would notice. Ernie charged after Goebel and made him admit that Illinois was offsides. Twenty minutes later, after the networks had signed off telling the nation that the game ended in a tie, the teams came back on the field as Ohio State was awarded one final play. Brown was toying with going for broke with a pass, but when his 17-year-old kicker, Johnny Stungis, pleaded to give him a shot, Brown relented. Stungis split the uprights from 33 yards out to give the Buckeyes a 29-26 win, despite the fact the nation thought it ended in a deadlock. It was a tough break for the networks, but our WTAM engineer managed to put the transmitter back on so I could inform at least Ohio that the Buckeyes had won."

In 29 years Manning watched all the great Buckeye players, from Gomer Jones and Warren Amling to Les Horvath and Vic Janowicz, but the greatest player he ever saw was Howard "Hopalong" Cassady. Manning rated Hop's pass interception in the 1954 Wisconsin game as the greatest clutch play he had ever seen, but he still had a spot in his heart for the 1944 18-14 Buckeye win over Michigan when Bill Willis came limping off the bench and Horvath literally picked the Bucks off the stadium turf to drive them to a last-period touchdown and the conference championship. "Tom Harmon was probably the greatest opponent to play here, but for a single-game performance I'll take J.C. Caroline of Illinois. In the 1953 Ohio State-Illinois clash, Caroline scored two touchdowns, set up several

more, and practically licked the Buckeyes single-handedly."

Much drama today is made of the announcement of the winner of the Heisman Trophy, awarded to the nation's top college player. Back in 1955, however, the announcement was made in between Hop Cassady's classes at Ohio State, and Manning was the man who made it. Even though the Heisman voting was to conclude at noon on November 29, 1955, Manning was

Manning on the set of his television show. *Photo courtesy of NBC*

WTAM had a true professional in Tom Manning. *Cartoon courtesy of Fred Reinert © 1954 **The Plain Dealer**; ad courtesy of Saegertown Beverages*

Manning was an accomplished after-dinner speaker who was honored many times for his long career in Cleveland. ***Photo courtesy of the author's collection***

so confident his favorite player would win that he had a special NBC nationwide hookup arranged for a 2 p.m. live broadcast on the OSU campus. Manning was right, because Cassady won the award and was informed by Ohio State president, Dr. Howard Bevis, in the president's office. Also on hand were Ohio Governor Frank Lausche and Coach Woody Hayes. Hayes was a big Manning booster. "That voice of his,"

Woody said, "which nature endowed him with, was the quality I thought of first. Next was his ability to draw word pictures. Whether he was signing off for Emerson Gill from the Golden Pheasant in the Hotel Hollenden, or giving away another carton of Wheaties for a home run blast at old League Park, he was always my favorite sports announcer. In 1954 we were practicing for Illinois on Friday afternoon, and he came on the field giving pep talks. I had to chase him away, telling him we like to play our games on Saturdays. In a profession that's constantly changing, Tom Manning remained on top for over 30 years. Yet he was a man of deep convictions and unchanging loyalties."

Cleveland Press columnist Franklin "Whitey" Lewis wrote a column about Manning on June 27, 1956, praising his longevity, his generosity, and his unique broadcast talents. In part, Lewis wrote, "In recent years Manning has become known as the unofficial coach of the Ohio State football team. During his broadcasts of the Buckeyes games, Tom has run more verbal broken field runs than Hopalong Cassady ever trod. He is an out-and-out rooter for Ohio State, and as such, has antagonized many listeners. But he carries right on, cheering the Bucks and sneering at the enemy as his public remains as divided as ever." Bob Hope, his longtime Cleveland friend, said Manning did more with a microphone and a gift of gab than just about anyone in the industry. "Whatever he's got, he should bottle it and sell it, and I'm first in line on the buying list."

"By present-day standards," John F. Royal said in 1956, "Tom Manning is a flop. The present-day sportscaster has to become the manager, the coach, and the umpire. I never heard Tom Manning double as an umpire or try to coach the Ohio State team. If you take that into consideration, he is a failure. But if you consider the people who listen, the great American audience, Tom is a great success. Not only as an announcer, but as a man."

As we concluded our 1967 interview, Manning, who had seen it all over a 44-year career, lamented the trend already building in the 1960s that flooded radio and television booths with ex-players. "Sports announcing

is an art," Tom said proudly, "and I don't believe that anybody should be given a microphone at a sporting event without having months of experience in a studio. The sponsors and stations idolize these athletes and hand them huge contracts based on image alone. These athletes are doing themselves and the nation that must listen to them a grave injustice." Manning cited, among others, Joe Louis, Rocky Marciano, and Sandy Koufax in that category. "Broadcasting to me has been a God-given privilege. It took me coast to coast and to Europe for the Olympics. I've been in the prize ring with the fighters, at home plate with the megaphone, and have interviewed every president of the United States back to 1925. I wouldn't change one single day of it. Radio has been a joy." Just over two years after our interview, on September 4, 1969, Tom Manning passed away, just a week before his 70th birthday.

While Tom Manning broadcast just about every sport under the sun in Cleveland and on the NBC network, from the Indians baseball games to the National Air Races to the All-American Soap Box Derby, he didn't broadcast professional football in Cleveland. The Cleveland Rams games were aired on WGAR, and Bob Kelley began broadcasting their games in 1937. Kelley, who also broadcast Notre Dame and then Michigan football during World War II, moved with the Rams to Los Angeles after the championship 1945 season and enjoyed a long career as voice of the Rams in L.A. He worked at KMPC from 1946 to 1964 and was regarded as one of the finest football announcers in the history of radio and television. "Ol' Kell' was the best football announcer I ever heard," longtime L.A. broadcaster Bud Furillo said. Kelley also announced the PCL's Angel games from 1948 to 1957 and was part of the first Angel aircrew in 1961. He also hosted a nightly talk show on KMPC. "His dinner-hour sports show made as many people gnash their teeth as cheer," columnist Jim Murray wrote. "But they listened. His mail was sulfuric. But they wrote."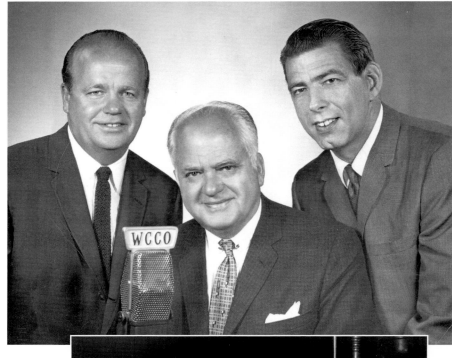

Kelley was born in Kalamazoo, Michigan, and attended high school in Elkhart, Indiana. He came to Cleveland to attend Western Reserve University where he graduated in 1942. He became the voice of Michigan football on WJR in 1942 and would hurry back to Cleveland to do the Rams game on Sunday. In 1964 Bob was carried out of the Los Angeles Coliseum during the annual Pro Bowl after a heart attack. The voice of the Rams died on September 9, 1966, at age 49.

(From left to right) Ray Scott, Halsey Hall, and Herb Carneal (above) were part of the WCCO team. Hall shared the duties at the Golden Gopher mike with Ray Christensen (below). *Background photo courtesy of Stew Thornley; foreground photo courtesy of Ray Christensen*

Halsey Hall enjoyed the same kind of reputation as Manning while broadcasting the fortunes of the Golden Gophers of Minnesota. Halsey, a combination of curmudgeon, poet, writer, and storyteller, made his first broadcast in 1923 on station WLAS, the forerunner of WCCO, while working on the sports staff of the *St. Paul Pioneer Press*. His first broadcast was recreating the Jack Dempsey-Tommy Gibbons heavyweight title fight in Shelby, Montana, on July 4, 1923. Halsey called the blow by blow from a second-floor window of the *Pioneer Press* building, shouting out the Western Union accounts of the bout through a megaphone to the

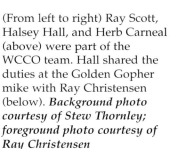

crowd of 2,500 below, because there was a great deal of local interest in Gibbons, a local boy from St. Paul.

In 1934 Halsey began broadcasting University of Minnesota football and Minneapolis Miller baseball. His salary was five dollars a game. Those were the Bernie Bierman years, and the 1934 Gophers, led by Pug Lund, Bud Wilkinson, and other All-Americans, were considered one of the great teams of all time. Minnesota went on to win five national championships in eight years. As the 1970s dawned, Halsey was still at the Gopher microphone, sharing duties with Ray Christensen, who broadcast Minnesota football for 50 years.

The son of a famous New York actress and a press agent, Halsey was born in New York City in 1898. The Hall family moved to Kansas City shortly after Halsey's birth, and when his parents split up so his mother could pursue her acting career, he accompanied his father to the Twin Cities, where, according to legend, young Halsey, nicknamed "Bundles" by his family, had to be spanked by his Dad to see his first Millers baseball game in 1909. The Millers played in the old American Association. "What a league it was," Halsey remembered. "From 1902 until the late 1950s there wasn't one change, the same eight teams for over 50 years. After seeing that first game in 1909, I fell in love with it. My dad had a season pass so I never missed a game until I entered World War I."

Halsey began his 41-year sportswriting career, which saw him report for five different papers, in 1919. He actually began covering Miller baseball in 1927, and over the years, he covered the exploits of Willie Mays, Ted Williams, Hoyt Wilhelm, and Carl Yastrzemski, among many others. Halsey was multifaceted,

Hall behind the mike for the Golden Gophers. *Photo courtesy of Stew Thornley*

refereeing NFL football for 10 years. He worked games involving the fabled Johnny Blood McNally, Cal Hubbard, and a quarterback who later coached named Curly Lambeau. "I worked the last game on the old Green Bay field and the first game at City Stadium and was in the booth when Lambeau Field was christened. I guess I've seen it all." Often Halsey would do double duty, officiating a game and then reporting on it in the paper and on radio the next day.

Halsey's most embarrassing moment as a football broadcaster came in a game at Michigan in Ann Arbor when Wes Fesler was coaching the Gophers. "We were sitting out under a canopy," Halsey recollected, "and when Michigan was teeing up the ball, I still hadn't taken the air. The station was running a commercial back at the studio. I was ranting and raving, 'For God's sake give me the microphone! To hell with that commercial!' The engineer just shrugged his shoulders, and in the meantime Michigan kicked off, and our halfback named Engel ran 98 yards for a touchdown. Then I got my cue. My opening words were, 'Good afternoon ladies and gentlemen, the Gophers are now lined up for the try for the point after touchdown.' The switchboard lit up back at the station, and the fans were all upset at me." Halsey Hall, curmudgeon and chronicler of a half-century of Minnesota sports as both a writer and a broadcaster, died on December 30, 1977, at age 79. All of Minnesota went into mourning.

Versatile Bill Slater was another veteran of early football broadcasting who also excelled as a commentator, narrator, author, and educator. A 1924 grad of the U.S. Military Academy at West Point, Slater chose education as his life's work and became an English and math teacher at his old high school in Parkersburg, West Virginia. Then came two years as Commandant at the Greenbrier Military School in Lewisburg, New York, before joining the faculty of the New York Military Academy at Cornwall-on-Hudson where he also coached football. After one year he headed west to lead the math department and to coach at the Blake School in Minneapolis. It was a math lecture at Blake that led Slater into radio. A pupil who was the son of a prominent radio executive in Minneapolis suggested to his father that Bill would be an excellent choice to announce football. "That boy's dad believed in making radio announcers just like they used to teach a kid to swim," Slater was quoted a few years later in a radio magazine. "He literally 'threw me in.'" His first assignment was a season-opening baseball doubleheader in which he talked for more than five hours non-stop. Soon came a three-year stint as the voice of University of Minnesota football. He got

his first network exposure broadcasting the 1933 Army-Navy game. With his technique behind the microphone earning him a solid reputation, Slater joined NBC in 1934. In 1936 he helped broadcast the Olympic games in Berlin, Germany. Away from sports he emceed several radio quiz shows and the popular *Breakfast at Sardi's*, which he was hosting when diagnosed with Parkinson's disease. Slater broadcast Yale-Penn football on the Atlantic Refining Co. network, and by 1936 had become the voice of the Paramount Newsreels. It was Slater who was broadcasting a pro football game when the first bulletin came that Pearl Harbor had been attacked on December 7, 1941:

"The Dodgers are ready to kick off now—They've just scored—Ace Parker did it—Jock Sutherland's boys lead the Giants 7-0. Here's the boot—it's a long one—down to around the three-yard line. Ward Cuff takes it, he's cutting up to his left, and he's over the 10—nice block there by Leemans. Cuff still going—He's up to the 25 and now he's hit and hit hard about the 27-yard line. Bruiser Kinard made the tackle…."

"WE INTERRUPT THIS BROADCAST TO BRING YOU THIS IMPORTANT BULLETIN FROM THE UNITED PRESS. FLASH-WASHINGTON. THE WHITE HOUSE ANNOUNCES JAPANESE ATTACK ON PEARL HARBOR. STAY TUNED TO STATION WOR FOR FURTHER DEVELOPMENTS, WHICH WILL BE BROADCAST IMMEDIATELY AS RECEIVED."

—Bill Slater

Track 18

Lindsey Nelson teamed with Mel Allen in 1953 to cover the college football season. *Photo courtesy of NBC*

In 1938, a young Jim Britt split the NBC college football broadcasts with Slater. "To Bill, announcing was a paid avocation," Britt said. "He was an amazing individual, and I learned a great deal from him. No one but an idiot could avoid learning from Bill. I remember when he was involved in one of the colossal mistakes in the history of radio. Assigned to broadcast a Cotton Bowl in Dallas, he arrived in the booth right at the kickoff. Looking out on the field, he couldn't tell which team was which, or the colors of each team's uniforms, or which of his spotters represented which team. For about the first three minutes of the game he had everything reversed. No one gave him any help at all. The two kids who served as spotters were totally confused. After discovering what he had done at the first commercial break, Bill simply confessed what had happened, that he had been caught in traffic, had not seen either team, and thought it was a very poor way to begin a broadcast, but if the audience would permit, he would like to start over again. And he did."

Mel Allen was first and foremost a baseball announcer, but he did his share of football broadcasting over the years. He began doing Yankee and Giants baseball games in 1939 and switched exclusively to the Yankees in 1946, where he remained until his firing late in the 1964 season.

Born Melvin Israel on Valentine's Day in 1913, he lived in several Alabama mining towns because his father's dry goods business took him from town to town. When his father sold the business, the Israels settled in Greensboro, North Carolina. Mel enrolled at the University of Alabama at age 15 and spent eight years on campus before graduating with a law degree in 1936. Besides serving as a student manager, young Mel served as PA announcer for Alabama home games before announcing Alabama and Auburn football for five dollars a game in 1935. Alabama coach Frank Thomas, who liked Mel's work on the PA, recommended him to a Birmingham station because he thought the handling of the PA system was the equivalent of broadcasting. Then came a trip to New York, an audition, and a part-time announcing job on the CBS network. Within two months he was switched from staff announcer to being the understudy to Ted Husing and Robert Trout, the two most eminent broadcasters in their fields. About this time he changed his last name to Allen, his father's middle name. His big break happened when he ad-libbed from an airplane for more than 50 minutes on the rain-delayed Vanderbilt Cup auto race. Soon after he was assigned

Mel Allen covered the Rose Bowl for NBC. *Photo courtesy of NBC*

to help Bill Dyer and France Laux announce the 1938 World Series. In 1939 he began broadcasting the fortunes of the Yankees and Giants, assisting Arch McDonald, because Larry MacPhail broke the longstanding radio ban in New York and installed Red Barber as voice of the Dodgers. Upon returning from the Army in 1946, Mel stuck exclusively with the Yankees and broadcast many of their historic exploits, including Don Larsen's perfect game in the 1956 World Series, which he considered the most thrilling game he ever broadcast.

Mel Allen broadcast several college football games and became synonymous with broadcasting the Rose Bowl. His most memorable was the 1963 classic in which Wisconsin came back from a 42-14 deficit under quarterback Ron Vanderkelen to lose 42-38 after having a touchdown called back. He worked many of the Rose Bowls with popular Southern California announcer Bill Symes. Another thriller was the 1956 battle between UCLA and Michigan State. "With the score tied 14-14, the ball on the Bruins' 31-yard line and 30 seconds to go, Spartan coach Duffy Daugherty decided to try a field goal," Mel remembered. "Sophomore Don Kaiser, who had never kicked a field goal, was sent in. To make things tougher, he had forgotten his contact lenses. Unable to see clearly, after he kicked the ball he had to turn around and watch the referee's signal to see if it was good. It was, and with seven seconds to spare, MSU clinched the victory 17-14."

Allen broadcast one season of Washington Redskins football in 1952 with Sammy Baugh completing his 16th and final season as the Redskins' quarterback. The team finished 4-8 under Curly Lambeau. Amoco Oil, the broadcast's sponsor, made Mel do a simulcast—

broadcasting on radio and television at the same time. Allen took plenty of heat being an outsider in Redskin territory. The following season, Mel was back in New York and never missed a beat. His uninterrupted tenure with the Yankees continued until 1964, and he covered other football assignments for NBC. Mel Allen died on June 16, 1996, at age 83.

Philadelphia's By Saam is another broadcaster who became a great baseball announcer but who began his career announcing football. A native Texan, By was broadcasting TCU football in 1935 for the Humble Oil Company, during the heyday of Sammy Baugh. On one afternoon, Ted Husing heard Saam doing a TCU game and was impressed. Husing recommended Saam to station WCCO in Minneapolis where he began broadcasting Minneapolis Miller games in 1937. He moved to Philadelphia in 1938, primarily to broadcast football, but began doing A's and Phillies' games too. Thirty-eight years later he retired from the booth and was awarded the Ford Frick Award in Cooperstown in 1990. Saam died on January 16, 2000, at age 85.

Announcers for the Atlantic Refining football network meet to plan the 1944 football season. In the front row on the left are By Saam and Bill Slater. In the second row on the left is Joe Tucker of Steeler fame and in the third row on the far right are Tom Manning and Les Quailey. *Photo courtesy of the author's collection*

A contemporary of Saam's, Connie Desmond, helped Red Barber broadcast the Brooklyn Dodgers but was also an accomplished football announcer. Desmond began his broadcasting career on his hometown station in Toledo, Ohio, WSPD in 1932. At first he hosted dance band remotes but soon was doing Mud Hen baseball. By 1942 he was in New York sharing the mike with Mel Allen on Yankees' and Giants' baseball. At the first meeting he attended of the New York Sports Broadcasters Association, Ted Husing introduced him and asked him what the news was from the Midwest. Connie thanked Husing and said, "The only prediction I can make is that Paul Brown will probably have a good football team this season." Husing looked at Connie and said, "Who is he?" Connie told him he had a great record at Massillon High and had taken over the coaching job at Ohio State. "I said you might be hearing from him one of these days. That fall Brown coached the Buckeyes to the national championship and went on to a legendary career as coach of the Cleveland Browns. Years later, Husing said, 'Brother, I should get all my information from neophytes who come out of Columbus, Ohio.'"

In the 1942 season, Connie and Mel Allen were assigned by Mutual to broadcast the Army-Navy classic, which, because of wartime travel restrictions, was played in Annapolis, with the Corps of Cadets not allowed to make the trip. Just their cheerleaders and the Army Mule made the trip. "I think it was the lowest attendance for an Army-Navy game since its inception when they played in a cornfield. The crowd was about 10,000. The Navy won their fourth straight over Army 14-0, and our broadcast was picked to be heard around the world on Armed Forces Radio. To maintain equality, the Midshipmen were asked to learn the Army songs, and this is where Mel and I both broke up, not only coast to coast, but all around the world. Half the Mids were sitting on the Army side, and there was an Army cheerleader, standing in front of the Navy brigade, leading them in chorus of 'On Brave Old Army Team.' Tears were coming down Mel's and my cheeks, we were laughing so hard. When the cue was given to take the air after a commercial I said, 'I don't know where you guys are in the fleet, but if you could see the sight now taking place before our eyes, you would die.' I looked for Mel to help me, and he was on the floor, crying he was laughing so hard. I regained enough composure to say, 'Let's go down and pick up the Army fight song as sung by the Navy Midshipmen.' Even though a war was going on, we received hundreds of telegrams from men in the Navy. Even with the horrors of war around them, these Annapolis grads were more concerned imagining themselves in a similar situation, not in front of the guns of the Japanese, but in front of the Army cheerleaders, singing, 'On Brave Old Army Team.'"

Desmond worked several years on the *CBS Football Roundup* with Red Barber hosting. "The Roundup concept came about in a conversation with Red," Connie said. "We thought, why should we stay with a game in which Notre Dame is whipping Iowa 56-0, when we could switch to a more exciting game? Red was scheduled to broadcast a Columbia-Navy game at Baker Field, and instead of listening to the band or doing an interview, we decided I would go to Dyche Stadium where Northwestern was playing Wisconsin and I would come on at halftime and describe what was happening in my game. It surprised everybody, including the other networks, so the next Saturday we decided to do three games, with Al Helfer joining our crew. Ernie Harwell followed. It was a giant success."

Leo Egan left his native Buffalo soon after the 1938 hurricane, landed in Boston, and spent 30 years doing both baseball and football. Egan replaced Ted Husing at Harvard Stadium after the CBS ace was banned for referring to Harvard quarterback Barry Wood as "putrid." Egan broadcast Harvard football during the Kennedy era when Bobby played for the Crimson. He was also at the mike when Ted Kennedy scored a touchdown against Yale. Perhaps Egan's top claim to fame was his originating the familiar phrase, "Atlantic keeps your car on the go." Atlantic sponsored Red Sox games and once, while recreating a game, Leo spontaneously thought up and delivered the expression over the air. He then promptly forgot about it. About a year later he attended an Atlantic announcers convention in New York during which time a new slogan was being unveiled. "When the curtain was pulled away and 'Atlantic keeps your car on the go' was revealed as the slogan, I nearly fainted. It seems an account exec heard me use the phrase and submitted it to his superiors. I was never able to press my claim and prove I first thought it up." Egan worked several baseball seasons with Jim Britt and was the first to announce a Boston baseball game live from the opposing team's ballpark—he did it in 1948 in Cleveland.

"Dutch" Reagan, otherwise known as Ronald Reagan and future president of the United States, began his radio career in 1932 with station WOC in Davenport, Iowa. He became sports director after vividly recreating the last quarter of an imaginary football game while sitting in a studio. "I picked a game that I'd played in, in college, the previous fall, which we'd won in the last 20 seconds by a 65-yard touchdown run," Reagan recalled in a 1984 interview. "I had everything, including the long blue shadows

Leo Egan broadcast Harvard football after Ted Husing was banned from Harvard Stadium. *Photo courtesy of WBZ Boston*

settling over the field, the chill wind coming in the open end of the stadium, and after 15 minutes, I called the winning touchdown for Eureka College."

Reagan's recreation was so convincing that when he finished, his clothes were wet with perspiration. It might have been an early-day example of method acting. His first assignment was broadcasting an Iowa game from Iowa City. He was so impressive that he received a 100 percent increase in pay, to $10 plus bus fare. "There were only three games left, but I was a

Ronald Reagan's career blossomed at WHO in Des Moines and his popularity led to his big-screen break. *Photo provided by Michael Rougier/Time Life Pictures/Getty Images*

sports announcer," Reagan said. "After all, if one buck for playing the game makes you a pro, $10 for talking it should, too."

Reagan soon switched to WOC's sister station in Des Moines, WHO, which was affiliated with NBC, and his career blossomed. He learned how to recreate baseball games from Chicago fixture Pat Flanagan, who became his mentor. In 1937 Reagan talked the heads of WHO into letting him accompany the Cubs to their spring camp on Catalina Island, near Los Angeles. Soon came his famous screen test, and sportscasting gave way to a movie career.

After his film career, Reagan went into politics and became the 40th President of the United States. He died June 5, 2004, from pueumonia at age 93.

Reagan's successor, the "Old Possum," Jim Woods, became famous as a baseball broadcaster in New York, Pittsburgh, Boston, and St. Louis, but the Kansas City native first made his mark in football. Woods declined to sign a contract with the St. Louis Cardinals in order to enroll at the University of Missouri. After six months he quit to take a job at a 100-watt station in Mason City, Iowa, where after two years he replaced Ronald Reagan, who had departed for Hollywood, as the voice of the Iowa Hawkeyes. The year was 1939, and Nile Kinnick and his fabled "Iron Men" were writing a unique chapter into the annals of midwestern football. "Fourteen men went the entire season," Woods recalled. "Kinnick was their leader, even though he was not an exceptional football player. He did have the ability to inspire others. Nile was one of the closest friends I lost in the war, flying to his death off a carrier. In 1939 we lost the one game to Tom Harmon and

Michigan, but outside of that it was tremendous. The 'Iron Men' captured the nation's fancy."

Notre Dame was a dominant power in the late 1930s and through the 1940s, yet Woods never saw them win a game. Beginning in 1939, he broadcast or watched the Irish in 12 games, and they never won any. "I broadcast two USC-Notre Dame games, both won by the Trojans, two Iowa upsets of the Irish, three

Michigan State upsets, a Pitt upset, and the 1931 USC victory when Johnny Baker kicked a game-winning field goal."

Jim Woods passed away on June 20, 1988.

Jim Britt was another pioneer who got his start doing Notre Dame football. Growing up in Detroit, he listened to Ty Tyson but was studying to become a

Jim Britt got his start in radio on a dare, and it led to a successful career describing the exploits of the gridiron Fighting Irish. He broadcast the first nationally televised football game in 1949. *Ad courtesy of the author's collection; photo courtesy of WOR Radio 710 NY, a Buckley Broadcasting station*

lawyer. It was 1933, and Gus Dorais was coaching the University of Detroit football team. After listening to a Titan broadcast, Jim kidded Gus about the poor effort on the radio broadcast.

"You think you can do a better job? " Gus asked.

"How could anyone do a poorer one?" Jim answered.

Several days later, Dorais called Jim and asked him to call the games. Jim was reticent, but Dorais dared him to try. "The next week I was broadcasting Detroit football, and without pay I might add." Two years later, bored with law and tired of selling insurance, Britt was hired on a small station in South Bend to broadcast Notre Dame football at the lofty salary of $50 a week. "I went into radio with everything I had," Britt said. "In the fall I took the examination all football referees are required to take. Not that I had to, but I wanted to know as much about the game as the fellows that handled it or played it."

In 1935, Britt broadcast one of the great games in college football history, the Ohio State-Notre Dame classic from Columbus. "Even though several network men were doing the game nationwide, I was the only voice going directly back to the home of the Irish. I managed to corral Grantland Rice as a halftime guest. The Buckeyes led 13-0 and dominated the first half, but Granny, though he didn't believe it for an instant,

offered a message of hope to the kids on the Notre Dame campus. He said, 'I don't think it can happen, but you never can tell about Notre Dame, can you?' The Irish came back to win 18-13 in miracle fashion."

The most strenuous broadcast Britt ever worked occurred when Notre Dame played Wisconsin at the old Randall Field in Madison. His booth, which sat alone on top of the stadium, resembled a Chick Sale outhouse. "We were able to fit two people into it before closing the door," Britt remembered. "I didn't think we were going to last the game out. I thought the shack was going to blow away. It was that flimsy."

His most difficult broadcast happened after his navy discharge in 1945 when Cornell hosted Bucknell in Ithaca. "There had been a polio scare at Bucknell so they were forced to take showers at halftime and wear fresh uniforms for the second half. I noticed right away someone had goofed, as Bucknell was wearing Cornell practice jerseys with completely different numbers. The equipment man had forgot to bring two sets of uniforms, so I spent the second half trying to figure out who was who, secretly wishing I was back in the navy getting shot at."

On another occasion, Britt was broadcasting a Yale-Brown game in New Haven. The field was soaked from three days of steady rain, so after about two minutes, as

> **"We were able to fit two people into it before closing the door, I didn't think we were going to last the game out. I thought the shack was going to blow away. It was that flimsy."** —Jim Britt

soon as they knocked heads, and spilled and slid in the turf, the players' numbers were indistinguishable. For the next 53 minutes, Yale and Brown set records for punting on first or second down. Conditions were that bad. "With about six minutes left in the game, Brown scored on a screen pass, and the player who caught the ball ran some 50 yards for the score," Britt remembered. "I had no idea who threw the ball or who caught it. Fortunately, there was a Boy Scout standing just outside our booth, which was across the field from the press box. I scribbled him a note, asking him to run down to the Brown bench and ask the coach who tossed the pass and who caught it. The score was 6-0, and I apologized to the audience for my failure to identify the players. The bedraggled Boy Scout returned with a minute left in the game, and we were just able to get the information on the air before signing off. Several newspapers the following day printed stories on how wonderful the Boy Scouts were."

Britt began broadcasting network football on the NBC Red chain in 1937. For $50 a game he was heard coast to coast on more than 300 stations, which adds up to about six cents a station. "When I began doing games for NBC, Ford Bond handled three quarters, and I did one. Then the following year I split the games equally with Bill Slater. In 1939 I handled the entire game with Ben Grauer handling the commercials and sidelights. When Army played Navy, I split the broadcast with Bill Stern."

In 1940 Britt joined the Yankee network as the voice of the baseball Braves and Red Sox, beginning a long career as a major league broadcaster. As a broadcaster he tried to be a good reporter. "Ty Tyson gave me one piece of advice I carried throughout my career: 'Report the game, don't play it.' In other words, don't make a 17-1 game a thrilling pitcher's duel. Bill Stern would have a 34-11 game in football a nail biter till the end. It was an insult to the intelligence of the listener, and the listener came first." Britt, who broadcast the first commercially televised college football game in 1949, passed away on December 28, 1980, at age 70.

Jack Brickhouse began his climb up the sportscasting ladder on station WMBD in Peoria, Illinois, in 1934. Six years later he had joined WGN in Chicago where he would reach the heights as the

Jack Brickhouse covered Bears football for WGN. *Photo courtesy of WGN Radio*

Brickhouse telecast more Bears games than any other sportscaster, including the 1963 and 1985 title seasons. *Photos courtesy of WGN Radio*

telecaster of Cubs baseball and Bears football. Jack's "Gee Whiz, Hey, Hey" style endeared him to Chicago sports fans. By that time his pay was much better than the $17 weekly salary he started at in Peoria as a part-time announcer and switchboard operator. "I was a better switchboard operator than announcer," Brickhouse admitted, "but I worked hard. If you worked 80 hours a week in those days, you were dogging it."

After a few months on the job, Brickhouse asked to broadcast the high school football games. At that time the station was paying a milkman five dollars to broadcast the games. "I wasn't much better than the milkman," Jack remembered. "I was so bad doing my first game another announcer hopped on a streetcar and came to my aid in the second half. I was going down for the third time when he arrived." Jack offered to resign, but station owner Edgar Bill felt Jack had promise and stuck with the young broadcaster. Six

Track 27

years later, Jack was on his way to Chicago and WGN.

When Bob Elson returned from military duty in 1945, Brickhouse was out of a job. He teamed with Steve Ellis to broadcast New York Giants baseball on station WMCA, and after one year returned to Chicago to do football and freelance. Then came television, and no one telecast more games than Brickhouse. He broadcast the Bears' title season of 1963 under George Halas and was still in the booth when the Mike Ditka-led Bears won in 1985.

Jack Brickhouse died on August 6, 1998, at age 82.

Philadelphia born Paul Douglas was a professional football player for the Frankford Yellow Jackets, which became the Philadelphia Eagles in 1933. He also played on the semi-pro Scranton Wasps before embarking on a career as a sports broadcaster. In 1941, the year Red Barber was voted the top play-by-play announcer, Douglas was picked the top sports commentator. He made his radio debut back in 1928 in Philadelphia, and after a year at Yale he returned home where he got work painting houses. After expressing dissatisfaction with a play-by-play baseball broadcast, Douglas auditioned at station WCAU, where he began as a staff announcer. After a year in Philadelphia he joined the CBS staff as a special-events sports announcer, and in 1935 began a long partnership with the Ligget and Myers Tobacco Company. Continuing to broadcast sports, along with announcing shows like Burns and Allen, Paul Whiteman, Jack Benny, and Fred Waring, Douglas also broadcast World Series and All-Star games. His popular on-air sports column series began in 1939. Douglas wrote and announced the program six

Paul Douglas played football semi-professionally before he covered sports in his radio column. *Photo courtesy of the author's collection*

days a week while also broadcasting sports on the Fox Movietone News.

In 1944, Douglas launched a long career in show business, first in nightclubs and then on Broadway as star of *Born Yesterday*.

Douglas was only 52 when he died on September 11, 1959.

Like many sportscasters of the early years, Stan Lomax began his career as a sportswriter. Beginning with the *Bronx Home News* in 1923, Lomax joined the

Stan Lomax broadcast college and professional football games in the early days of the emerging sport for WOR. *Left photo courtesy of Westwood One; right photo courtesy of WOR Radio 710 NY, a Buckley Broadcasting Station*

New York Journal a few years later to cover the Brooklyn Dodgers. On an off day during the 1930 baseball season, Tommy Brooks, in charge of the Hearst papers radio division, recruited both Stan and fellow beat writer Ford Frick, to broadcast sports. The station was WGBS, owned by the Gimbel Brothers department store. For several years, Stan wrote baseball and did a daily radio show. When the *Journal* merged with the *American* into one newspaper, he left sportswriting to concentrate on radio. He joined WOR where his nightly radio show ran for over than 30 years.

Besides his show, Lomax did play-by-play football on both the pro and college level. "On one occasion in 1933 I was broadcasting a pro football game between the Brooklyn Dodgers and the Pittsburgh Pirates, before they became the Steelers, and we had to leave the air, no matter what, at five o'clock for a live broadcast," recalled Lomax. "The outcome of the game hinged on a field-goal attempt in the closing seconds by Pittsburgh. If it was good, then the Pirates would tie the game 3-3. Just as the kick sailed into the air, I was cut off by the network leaving the outcome a mystery to all those who had listened to the broadcast." The kick was good.

Stan did plenty of football over the years. For seven seasons he was the voice of Army football, plus did Big Ten football as well as Brooklyn Dodger pro football in

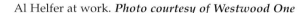

Al Helfer at work. *Photo courtesy of Westwood One*

both the NFL and the AAFC. After more than 50 years in broadcasting, Stan Lomax retired in the mid-1970s. He was 89 years old when he passed away in 1988.

Al Helfer was another pioneer who played the game of college football. Born and raised in the coal mine country of western Pennsylvania, Al played on the Washington and Jefferson team coached by the immortal Wilbur "Fats" Henry, a member of the first class of the Pro Football Hall of Fame. Al also served as sports director of the local radio station. His first big job was on Pittsburgh station WWSW, owned by the *Post-Gazette* newspaper, in 1932. He did Pitt Panther and Carnegie Tech football, two teams he had faced as a 180-pound fullback. "It was in 1934 that I broadcast what many consider the greatest football game ever played, Minnesota against Pitt," Al recounted. "The Golden Gophers, led by halfback Pug Lund, beat the Panthers 13-7. Bernie Bierman's '34 Gophers rank at the top of the list of greatest teams with stars such as Lund, Bud Wilkinson, Phil Bengston, Milt Bruhn, and Babe LeVoir. The Gophers gave a great display of defense in the first quarter when Pitt recovered a fumbled punt on Minnesota's six-yard line and wound up on the 12 after four plays. Pitt had its own star in Marshall Goldberg. Pitt coach Jock Sutherland called it the greatest game between the two greatest teams that ever played on the same field."

Helfer also recreated Pirates games from the Western Union code because the Pirates' brass banned live broadcasts from Forbes Field.

Helfer moved to Cincinnati in 1935 to team with Red Barber on Reds broadcasts and then joined CBS in New York in 1937 where he did everything from

Russ Hodges and partner Ernie Harwell in the press box (above). Hodges's coverage of the Washington Redskins on WOL made him one of the local football greats. *Photo provided by United Press International; ad courtesy of WOL*

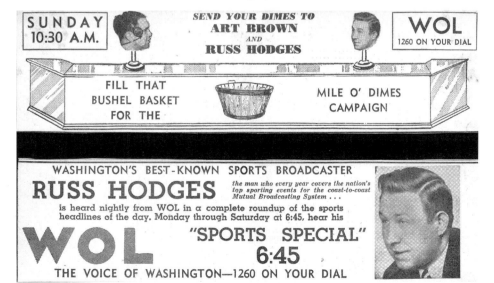

football to announcing for *The Hit Parade, Famous Jury Trials,* and *Charlie Chan*. He and Red also pioneered daily baseball broadcasts in 1939 when Larry MacPhail took over the Brooklyn Dodgers.

Helfer became great friends with Ted Husing. "When I did the Notre Dame-Carnegie Tech game in 1935 for Mutual, Ted helped me a great deal while others were trying to cut me up because I was new. Ted accepted me and even asked me to be his halftime guest so as to introduce me to his CBS audience. I, in turn, asked him to come over to say hello to my listeners on the Mutual network. Husing even served as my spotter on one occasion. Upon discharge from the navy, my first assignment was a Brooklyn Dodger-Green Bay Packer game at Ebbets Field. I was still in my navy uniform, on terminal leave. We were having problems locating a spotter, and when Tom Gallery, then the Dodger general manager, heard about our plight, he told us he'd find us a spotter. About an hour before the game I was preparing when Ted Husing came down the ladder. I thought he was kidding when he said he was my spotter. 'No, I'm not Al,' said Ted. 'You've been gone five years, and the game has changed. This is your first broadcast back, and you're not going to make a mistake.' He wouldn't let me reveal he was in the booth,

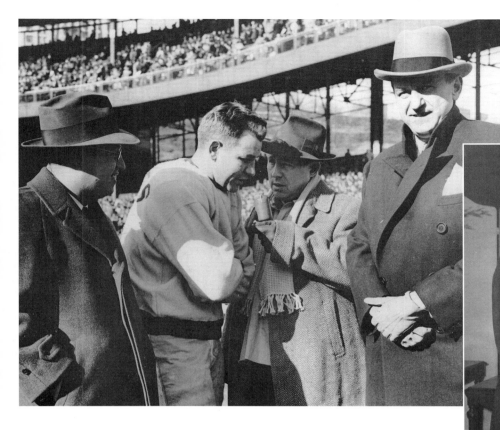

Left: Hodges (holding mike) interviews Redskin Tuffy Leemans as Redskin owner George Preston Marshall (right) stands by. Below: Arch McDonald shakes hands with Hodges. *Background photo provided by United Press International; foreground photo courtesy of WTOP*

because he was under contract to CBS, and I was working that day for NBC."

Helfer, who emceed the Heisman Trophy dinner from the Downtown Athletic Club in New York for 24 years, died on May 16, 1975, at age 63.

In Washington, the roll call of football announcing greats included Russ Hodges, Harry Wismer, Arch McDonald, Bob Wolff, and Jim Gibbons. Born in 1910 in Dayton, Tennessee, Hodges grew up in Danville, Kentucky, where he served as the water boy for Bo McMillan's "Praying Colonels" of Centre College, a team that became legendary for its upsets of bigger schools in the late 1910s and early 1920s. Offered a scholarship to play football at Kentucky, the young halfback suffered a career-ending ankle injury during his sophomore year and ended up in the broadcast booth, first as a spotter, and then as the play-by-play man in 1930 at WHAS, Louisville. After stops in Rock Island, Illinois, where he broadcast Iowa football; Chicago, and Charlotte, Russ landed in Washington, D.C. in 1943 where he assisted McDonald on Senators baseball and did football for the Redskins. Russ left Washington in 1946 to join Mel Allen on the Yankee broadcast. He became the voice of baseball's New York Giants in 1949 and stayed until his death in April 1971.

Arch McDonald was primarily a baseball announcer but did his share of Redskins and local college games. On his scoreboard show he created a fictitious team called Hedgemore that played such teams as Almost Normal, Comatose State, Gremlin U., International Correspondence School, Electoral College, Hampden Kidney, and Hackwith U. He gave the Hedgemore scores for years on the air. Hedgemore, of course, never lost.

Jim Gibbons broadcast Redskins football for 25 years. At first Gibbons was the color man to Harry Wismer from 1944 to 1951, and then in 1952 he assisted Mel Allen in his one season with the Redskins. Gibbons then moved up to play by play. In 1960 he began doing the Redskins on television and finished up in the late 1960s on radio. Gibbons was also one of the many who broadcast Notre Dame football. He did it 17 years to be exact.

Likeable and admired, Gibbons was revered in Washington. Longtime Washington columnist and broadcaster Mo Siegel used to say, "There must be something wrong with Gibbons—everybody likes him." Gibbons died in April 2001 at age 87.

The West Coast has provided some great football voices over the decades, among them Ernie Smith of San Francisco, who announced Seals and Mission Reds minor league baseball on station KYA and was long synonymous as the voice of the East-West Shrine game. Smith, one of the top tackles of his era, earned All-America first-team honors at USC in 1932, playing on a pair of national champion and Rose Bowl-winning teams. A world-class swimmer at USC, Smith played four seasons for Curly Lambeau in Green Bay in the 1930s. Smith died in 1985 at age 75.

Other West Coast greats include Ken Niles, Jack Keough, Braven Dyer, Don Wilson, Mike Frankovich, Ken Carpenter, Bob Kelley, Sam Balter, Bud Foster, Don Thompson, Bill Symes, Bob Fouts, Lon Simmons ◎, Gil Stratton, Dick Enberg, Tom Kelly, Bill King, and

Gil Stratton, the voice of the Rams. *Photo courtesy of the author's collection*

◎ Track 33

Keith Jackson. Keough was the pioneer announcer of station KPO in San Francisco and became well known throughout the Bay area for his colorful play-by-play reporting. Keough was also responsible for Don Thompson's start in sportscasting. Ernie Smith said, "Jack's misfortune was to fail to show up in 1928 for a Shrine East-West broadcast, because New Year's Day was too soon after New Year's Eve. Thompson, who was supposed to be his spotter was pressed into service and gave a great performance. He was still at it 42 years later."

Gil Stratton was a Hollywood actor before becoming the voice of the Rams in the late 1950s. His most notable role was Cookie in the William Holden World War II prison camp classic, *Stalag 17*. Gil grew up in Brooklyn and broke into show business in 1939 as one of the stars of the Broadway play, *Life with Father*. He also starred with June Allyson and Nancy Walker in the musical *Best Foot Forward*. After serving as a bombardier in the Army Air Corps during World War II, he landed in Hollywood where he sang "Embraceable You" with Judy Garland in *Girl Crazy*. Gil worked with Gale Storm on radio's *My Little Margie* and in the mid-1950s played Eddie Mayehoff's nerdy son on the television series, *That's My Boy*.

However, sports were Gil's first love, and for nine seasons he umpired professional baseball on the West Coast, working his way up to the Pacific Coast League. In 1955 he became the voice of the Rams on CBS television, announcing the fabled Rams of Norm Van Brocklin and Crazy Legs Hirsch. "My favorite players

Gil Stratton and Eddie Mayehoff on *That's My Boy* in 1955. **Photo courtesy of CBS**

were Dick Bass, the Guvnor, who wore spats and a homburg, and Jon Arnett, whom I nicknamed 'Jaguar Jon,' in hopes we'd get a free car. It didn't happen."

Now 82, Gil and his wife, Dee, continue to live in Toluca Lake, California, just about a half mile from where one of his movies, *The Wild One*, starring Marlon Brando, was filmed.

Bob Fouts and Lon Simmons were long known as the voices of the 49ers. Fouts, who handled the telecasts, imparted his knowledge of the game to son Dan, who became a Pro Football Hall of Famer with the Chargers and outstanding color man in his own right.

For a while Dan served as a statistician for his dad. Dan had his aspirations for playing end when trying out for Pop Warner football, but Bob was quite adamant that he should learn to play quarterback. Bob said it was the only football advice he ever gave his son.

Simmons joined station KSFO in 1957 and became the radio voice of the 49ers as well as teaming with Russ Hodges on Giants baseball. He lasted more than 40 years on both jobs, chronicling the 49ers from the days of Y.A. Tittle to John Brodie to Steve Spurrier to Jim Plunkett to Joe Montana. In 1981, he gave way to his successor, Don Kline. Lon came back to the Niners in the late 1980s and was at the mike when Montana executed his famous drive, throwing a last-second pass to John Taylor to sink the Bengals 20-16 in Super Bowl XXIII.

"Yours truly," Don Wilson, Jack Benny's affable pitchman who possessed radio's most famous belly laugh, won his early radio fame as a football broadcaster for KFI in Los Angeles in the late 1920s and 1930s. In the 1934 Rose Bowl game, Wilson shared the microphone with Ken Carpenter, who later became famous as the spokesman for Kraft cheese. It was after the 1934 Rose Bowl that NBC programming chief, John F. Royal, brought Wilson to New York for other top sports assignments and emcee work, including the Benny show. ◎

Ken Carpenter, whose sports announcing career was somewhat short lived and confined almost entirely to football, also did the play by play on the Rose Bowl games of 1934, 1935, and 1936, sharing the mike with Don Thompson of the NBC staff in San Francisco.

A native of Avon, Illinois, Carpenter moved to Hollywood in 1929 and shortly became a staff announcer for KFI radio. As a staff announcer at KFI, Carpenter broadcast USC and UCLA football for the Pacific Coast and the NBC network from 1932 through 1935, alternating quarters with staff announcer Tom Hanlon. From 1938 to 1942 he served as color man for Bill Stern on all NBC originations from Los Angeles, including the Rose Bowl. "Those Rose Bowl games were a big break for me," Carpenter recalled, "as they made me known to clients and advertising agencies in the East, so I had a jump on other local men when the big commercial shows started originating in L.A. in the mid-1930s." Carpenter became Bing Crosby's announcer in 1936 shortly after Bing took over hosting duties on the Kraft Music Hall. Carpenter sold more Kraft cheese than most grocery stores as he remained with Bing for the next 27 years. Ken Carpenter died on October 16, 1984, at age 84.

Tom Kelly's career as the voice of USC Trojan athletics is in its fifth decade. He began calling Trojan football and basketball games in 1961, beginning on radio and then on TV since 1989. Kelly has described five USC national championship teams, and all of the great backs, including Mike Garrett, O.J. Simpson, Charles White, Anthony Davis, and Marcus Allen; five Heisman Trophy winners; and 85 first-team All Americans.

Kelly's career began in Ashland, Wisconsin, where he was injured playing football at Northland College. Then came stops in Duluth, Minnesota; Des Moines, Iowa; and Peoria, Illinois, before coming to Los Angeles. He also did play by play for the San Diego Chargers and USFL Los Angeles Express.

◎ **Track 11**

Dick Fishell is a good example of a pioneer sportscaster who made it big on both coasts. As a football player at Syracuse and for two seasons in the NFL in 1933 and 1934 with the Brooklyn Dodgers, Fishell joined WMCA in New York as sports director in 1935. Besides a nightly sports show, he did the entire Columbia University football schedule in 1935. In 1936 he announced all of the Princeton games and broadcast major track meets and bike races from Madison Square Garden and the National Tennis Championships from Forest Hills. In 1937 Fishell joined WHN as sports director and obtained the exclusive rights to the New York Giants football games. From 1937 through 1941, Fishell did the play by play of Giants home and away football games. On December 7, he was broadcasting the Giants-Dodgers football game at the Polo Grounds in competition with Bill Slater. "At the end of the first quarter our phone from the studio rang and gave the news item that I announced on the air. It read: 'The Japanese have bombed Pearl Harbor.'" Fishell was commissioned into the Marine Corps in September 1942, and after three years of service—15 months of which were spent in the Pacific—he was discharged. "Two days later I was on the air at the Los Angeles Coliseum doing play by play of the USC football game." He then started a nightly sports show on KFWB in Hollywood and in 1946 became the play-by-play announcer of the Los Angeles Dons football games in the old All-America Football Conference. After describing the action of practically every major sport from 1936 through 1947, Fishell retired from broadcasting to form his own public relations business.

Eddie Dooley was a contemporary of Fishell in New York. Dooley edited the top college football magazine in the country, *Illustrated Football Annual*, in the 1930s and later became New York State Boxing Commissioner. Dooley broadcast for the Revelation Tobacco Company over the Mutual Network in New York, Chicago, and Detroit. He also hosted shows for Shell Oil on station WOR and for Chesterfield and Royal Typewriter on CBS.

Six-foot, eight-inch Gene Kelly rivaled Jack Drees as the tallest sportscasters in history. Primarily based in Philadelphia in the 1950s, Gene also did Cincinnati

Eddie Dooley went into radio after editing *Illustrated Football Annual*. **Photo courtesy of WOR Radio 710 NY, a Buckley Broadcasting Station**

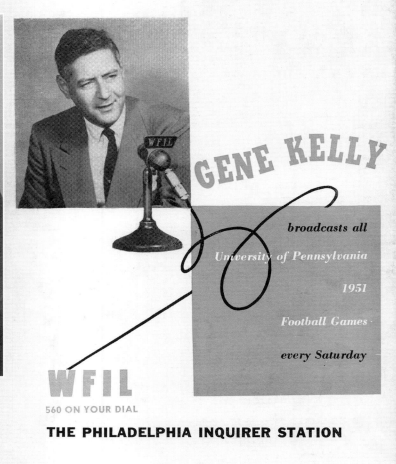

Gene Kelly (right), with Robin Roberts (left) and Jim Learning (middle), towered above his contemporaries. *Photo courtesy of the author's collection; ad courtesy of WFIL*

Reds baseball in the 1960s. His football play-by-play experience began at his alma mater, Marshall College, in 1939 when he broadcast a Buckeye Conference game between Cam Henderson's Thundering Herd and Miami of Ohio. He would later broadcast games for Notre Dame, Purdue, Penn State, Indiana, Syracuse, and the Ivy League. In 1964 he broadcast St. Louis Cardinal football over KMOX. He also teamed with Bill Slater to broadcast the Indy 500 from 1946 through 1949. Communicating with "warmth and heart" was Kelly's trademark. "There are not many guys in our racket who have more than 'tinny warmth.'"

Gene Kelly passed away on September 18, 1979.

For more than 30 years, Kern Tips was the voice of the Southwest Conference. An executive at advertising agency Wilkinson-Schiwetz and Tips, which later merged with McCann-Erickson advertising agency, Tips began broadcasting when the Humble Oil Company began sponsoring Southwest Conference games.

Born in Houston in 1904, Kern attended Texas A&M and Rice. While at Rice, he began writing sports for the *Houston Post* and then the *Chronicle*, becoming sports editor in 1926, a job that lasted through 1934. He began his long association with radio in the crystal set days of

Track 62

1926 as a sports reporter. He had a regular program by 1930. He served as general manager of Houston station KPRC from 1935 through 1946.

Kern spent 32 years broadcasting Southwest Conference football, beginning in 1934 and ending after the 1966 season. A stickler for detail, Kern had a breezy style but he was totally prepared. Coaches took him into their confidence and briefed him on anything new to expect. Bill Sansing, appointed the first sports information director at the University of Texas in 1946, said Kern was extraordinarily intelligent. "He also had the fastest eye-voice coordination I've ever seen," remembered Sansing, who resides today in San

Antonio. "It was uncanny. Kern described it as fast as he saw it. There was no lag time. He didn't even need a spotter." Sansing said Kern was totally prepared, even though he did the games mostly as a hobby, since he had a full-time job at the ad agency. "He had a deep, resonant voice. He could go anywhere in Texas, and

Humble network executive Bill Sansing, ad man Joe Wilkinson, and announcer Kern Tips took the Southwest Conference by storm. *Photo courtesy of Bill Sansing; ad courtesy of Exxon Mobil Corporation*

Go to the Games
WITH HUMBLE

This fall, drive to as many football games as you can. You'll enjoy them, every one . . . And you'll find your trip extra pleasant if you service your car under our Humble sign before you start.

When you can't see the game of your choice, tune in one of Humble's broadcasts of Southwest Conference football games. Again this year, the Southwest's top announcers will bring you vivid, play-by-play descriptions direct from Southwest Conference stadiums. You'll enjoy every second, from tense start to exciting finish . . . Follow the best football in the U. S.; go to the games with Humble.

KERN TIPS, ace sports announcer of the nation. Chief of Humble's football announcing staff since 1935.

CHARLIE JORDAN, popular wherever football is talked and listened to in the Southwest. Charlie takes you right into the stadium with him.

VES BOX, leading sports commentator of Dallas. A keen follower of all sports, Ves' vivid descriptions of Southwest Conference games have established his reputation as one of the best sports announcers in the country.

BILL MICHAELS, of San Antonio, is a sports writer turned broadcaster. His accurate descriptions of play please the well-informed follower of football.

people would recognize his voice after just a few words," remembered Sansing, who joined the ad agency in 1949 and worked with Tips until Tips's death in 1967. "He would work on his dozen 'ad libs,' such as turning 'sixes into sevens,' for each game and had a wonderful knack for turning a phrase."

Kern's color man for years on the Humble network was Alec Chesser, who joined the team after the war. The color man in those days basically did the preview, the halftime, and the postgame with an occasional comment during the game. "Bill Wilkinson was a stickler for adhering to the game description," Sansing said. "Kern couldn't mention injuries or anything controversial. One time at Ownby Stadium in Dallas when the SMU Mustangs hosted Texas A&M in an important game, the game was stopped for 15 minutes because a section of bleachers collapsed under the weight of the big crowd. There were several injuries. Kern kept talking but never once mentioned the incident."

In 1959 Tips was selected as the man who contributed most to radio and television in Texas by the Association of Broadcasting Executives in Texas and was the recipient of the only award ever made by the Southwest Football Officials Association for distinguished service to the sport. For five straight years he was voted Texas Sportscaster of the Year. It was a sad day throughout Longhorn country when Kern Tips died of cancer on August 3, 1967. He was 63 years old.

Connie Alexander had the tough assignment of taking over for Tips. Other announcers of note in the state of Texas were Ves Box, Charlie Jordan, Bill Michaels, Eddie Barker, John Ferguson, and current ESPN broadcaster Ron Franklin.

Just a chosen few of the golden voices from radio's heyday are still active in the new century. Bob Wolff still has his own show on Long Island cable. Wolff began as Arch McDonald's assistant doing Senators baseball games in Washington, became their number-one broadcaster, and moved with the team to Minnesota in 1961. A graduate of Duke University, Wolff began broadcasting on WDNC in Durham during his sophomore year in college. While serving in the Solomon Islands during World War II, he wrote a pamphlet voicing his displeasure with some of the aspects of the overseas war effort and suggested some needs for change. He mailed his critique to the War Department and a few weeks later received orders to report to the Department of the Navy in Washington. He felt he would either be commended or court martialed. Fortunately, it was the former, and he was placed in charge of writing training books and movies. At war's end, Wolff remained in Washington and became the first television sportscaster in the city. At the tender age of 25, he began televising Senators baseball and spent 14 years with the club in either the radio or TV booth.

In the early 1950s Wolff broadcast a college and NFL Game of the Week on the old Dumont Network. He also did a Mutual Network college Game of the Week, working with Ted Husing and Bill Stern. All together, Wolff broadcast 12 Gator Bowls, two Sugar Bowls, and two Rose Bowls. "On New Year's Day in 1965 I broadcast Michigan's 34-7 win over Oregon State in the Rose Bowl and flew back immediately to do the Michigan-Princeton game in the holiday basketball

Bob Wolff in the press box. *Photo courtesy of Bob Wolff*

Wolff interviews the great Vince Lombardi in 1966. *Photo courtesy of Bob Wolff*

festival at Madison Square Garden when Cazzie Russell matched up with Bill Bradley."

Wolff announced two of the most memorable games in sports history, both of them occurring at Yankee Stadium in New York. The first was on October 8, 1956, when he broadcast the last four innings of Don Larsen's World Series perfect game against the Dodgers. A little over two years later, from a different vantage point at Yankee Stadium, Wolff described pro football history as the Baltimore Colts defeated the New York Giants in the first overtime championship game in NFL history. Johnny Unitas directed a last-second drive to tie the game on Steve Myhra's field goal, and then Unitas engineered the winning drive in overtime capped by Alan Ameche's touchdown to win it 23-17. There were several broadcasts of the game, both TV and radio. Wolff was working the game on radio with Baltimore's Bailey Goss on the Colts network sponsored by National Bohemian beer. Chuck Thompson was doing the telecast with Chris Schenkel. "At halftime I remember putting my 19-year-old statistician on the air, asking him what he thought of the game. His name was Maury Povich."

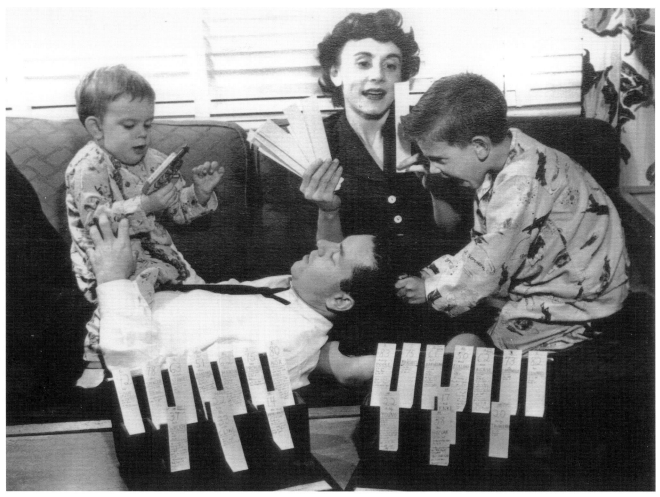

Wolff is quizzed on players' numbers for the 1953 Colts-Lions game
by his wife, Jane, while his sons play. ***Photo courtesy of Bob Wolff***

Wolff accompanied the Senator franchise to Minnesota in 1961, and when Lindsey Nelson left NBC to join the fledgling Mets expansion team in 1962, he replaced him as Game of the Week telecaster along with Joe Garagiola. They worked together for three seasons until Bob joined Madison Square Garden where he spent many years doing televised Knicks and Rangers games along with top college basketball games at the Garden.

Ted Husing

The Big Three, Part Two

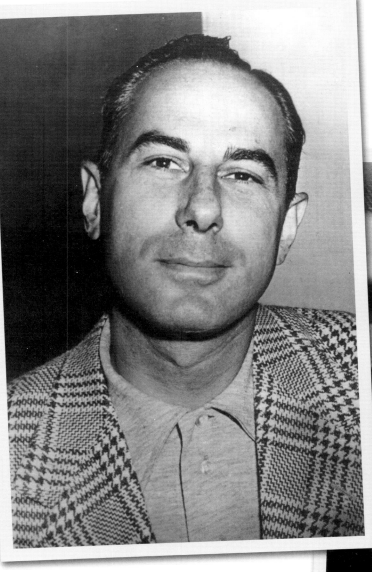

Bill Stern

Harry Wismer

As radio was shaping into a national phenomenon through the popular voices of Graham McNamee, Ted Husing, and Bill Munday, there were three men who helped usher in the golden age of radio. Ironically, the middleman in the first Big Three extended his career to become the first of the second Big Three. Ted Husing, Bill Stern, and Harry Wismer would bring football to gridiron glory on the airwaves and make it a nationwide pastime that has gone on to become one of the most lucrative businesses on the field and on the television screen. Their personalities and popularity with listeners allowed them to bring the games to life and give the radio fans the best seat in the house.

By the mid-1930s, Ted Husing was riding the crest of his sportscasting career. He was Mr. CBS, adept at every sport, far outshining the field on everything from college football to the Olympic games. His two main competitors from radio's early days, Graham McNamee and Bill Munday, lacked Husing's staying power. In fact Munday had disappeared from the national scene many years earlier.

When the popularity, and more importantly the health, of McNamee began to wane in the late 1930s, NBC was forced to find a replacement. They didn't conduct a nationwide search for their new number-one sportscaster. Instead, his hiring came about in almost a strange way, as strange as some of his tall tales he told on his Colgate Newsreel program. Bill Stern was a brash rich kid from Rochester, New York, who bounced in and out of several prep schools before landing at Pennsylvania Military College in 1925. His rise to broadcasting heights was truly as dramatic as some of his descriptions. ◎

Theatrics interested Stern more than radio, and his first real job after graduation in 1930 was as an usher at the new Radio City Music Hall in New York. "I had gone out to Hollywood to try and get a job as an actor and wound up digging cement postholes," he recounted about his first real job, which he quit after three days. From usher, Bill moved up to stage manager at Radio City. The radio bug was about ready to bite him. The NBC studios were directly across the street from the Music Hall, and young Bill constantly plagued program boss John F. Royal for a job. Royal finally relented and let Stern accompany McNamee to a 1934 Navy-William and Mary game in Baltimore. Royal felt by giving Stern a few minutes on the air he would hang himself and disappear. It was the only way Royal felt he could get Stern off his back. With two minutes left in a tense, scoreless game and Navy driving, McNamee handed Bill the microphone. He did well, and a surprised Royal let him accompany McNamee for the final two games of the season. His work drew the attention of *New York Mirror* columnist Nick Kenny:

"Maybe it's because Stern played football with Pennsylvania Military and was quarterback that his broadcasts are so interesting. He is interested in what is happening on the gridiron and nothing else. And that's how the radio fans feel. Stern lets the drama of the game itself hold the emotion of the listeners. He loves the game too well to garnish it with synthetic excitement. Stern really gives you a play-by-play description of the game. Keep it up, Bill!"

Kenny's statements are a bit surprising, because Stern got the reputation of putting drama over accuracy on his play by play. When Stern hired an agent to negotiate a contract with Royal and NBC,

Royal fired him and he ended up getting a football job in Louisiana. While driving back from one of those games, the Texas-Centenary game on October 20, 1935,

Stern had a sense of drama and confidence that carried him through the ups and downs of his career. *Photo courtesy of the author's collection*

Stern was involved in a high-speed car crash that cost him a leg. "I shouldn't have lost the leg," Stern said. "It was a compound fracture, but the doctor operating on me didn't clean out the wound. Sand, gravel, cement, and even manure had rubbed itself into the wound. As a result, gangrene set in, and my left leg had to be amputated. When I woke up from the surgery and my leg was gone, it was the greatest shock of my life. I was horrified."

Stern was traumatized over the chain of events. Brought back to a hospital in New York, he had lost his will to live. Upon being told of Bill's condition, John Royal hopped a cab to the hospital, grabbed a breakfast tray from a nurse leaving his room, and said, almost without thinking, "How are you going to broadcast next year's football for NBC if you don't eat?" That gave Stern the inspiration to get well.

Six months later he came to Royal on crutches to tell him he had taken a $75-a-week job at WHO in Des Moines, Iowa. "I reminded Royal's assistant, Phil Carlin, of what Mr. Royal had said about a job with NBC. He told me to sit still and went into Royal's office. A few minutes later Carlin came out and said, 'Mr. Royal remembers his offer. You're not going to Des Moines, you're staying here to do football for us.' And that's how I got back to NBC."

Stern joined the NBC sports team that included Bill Slater and Don Wilson. By late 1936 he had moved into the number-one sports job. "I got some great games that season. The Yale-Princeton game at Palmer Stadium, which Yale with Clint Frank and Larry Kelly won 26-23, still stands out as one of the most thrilling contests I've ever seen. This game gave me my first chance to demonstrate what I could do under extreme pressure and excitement." One of his first big assignments was to broadcast the 1937 Sugar Bowl. His prime ambition was to broadcast the Rose Bowl, but eastern announcers were refused the position on the grounds they were too flowery. This stemmed from the 1927 Rose Bowl when Graham McNamee spent more time talking about the scenery than the game. Two years later, in 1939, the committee relented, and Bill broadcast his first of 10 Rose Bowls, calling it the most "unbelievable game I ever witnessed." Unbeaten, untied, and unscored-upon Duke was leading Southern Cal 3-0 with two minutes left, when a fourth-string quarterback named Doyle Nave, who had played only 28 minutes the entire season, entered the game for USC along with third-string end Al Krueger. Nave promptly threw four passes to Krueger, the last being a 14-yard scoring pass with 41 seconds left to give the Trojans a stunning 7-3 victory. For 599 minutes and 19 seconds, Duke had not given up a point, but with 41 seconds

Buck Canal (above, second from the right) and Stern cover football for NBC, and Stern (below, left) interviews a Notre Dame football player. *Top photo courtesy of NBC; bottom photo provided by Mark Kauffman/Time Life Pictures/Getty Images*

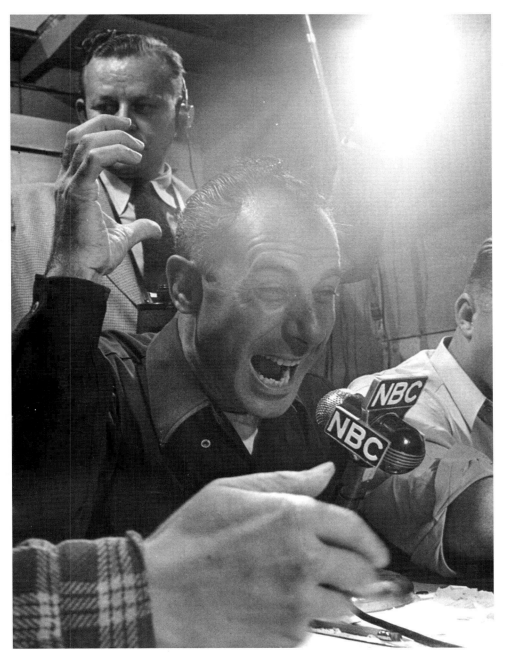

Stern's flair for the dramatic takes over as he covers the Notre Dame-Illinois game in 1946. *Photo provided by Mark Kauffman/Time Life Pictures/Getty Images*

left saw their unblemished mark topple as they lost the game on the only score they gave up all season.

In his career Stern announced five Sugar Bowl games and three Cotton Bowl classics. He never cared who won as long as he kept the audience. "I knew if somebody tuned in and I said the score was 35-7, they would tune right out again. So I wouldn't give the score, instead trying to create as much excitement as I could." Stern's penchant for creating drama rankled more sedate broadcasters such as Jim Britt. "One Saturday afternoon I was driving back to Boston from New Haven after a game at the Yale Bowl and flipped on the radio to hear Stern describe the last few minutes of the Purdue-Indiana game for the Old Oaken Bucket. With 48 seconds to play I nearly drove off the road when I heard Stern say, 'The score is Indiana 34, Purdue 11. If Indiana can hold this lead for the next 48 seconds, they'll win the game.' To me this type of reporting is ridiculous. I thought it was an insult to the intelligence of the listener, and after all, the listener should come first."

For several years Stern and Ted Husing waged a battle for network supremacy that bordered on fanatical. Husing left no doubt that he felt Stern was an imitator. On one occasion, after a Notre Dame game in South Bend, both announcers were waiting for the train to New York when Bill complimented Ted on the sports jacket he was wearing. Husing, remaining aloof, said sarcastically,

"My God, Stern, now are you going to start copying my clothes, too?" On another occasion, Stern barely avoided serious trouble in trying to upstage Husing. They were both doing the Illinois-Army game in Champaign, and the NBC and CBS booths were side by side high above the stadium. Both networks' cable lines ran along a narrow ledge in front of the booths. On an impulse, Stern found some cutting pliers in the engineer's bag, crawled out on the narrow ledge, and snipped what he thought were Husing's lines. It never occurred to him that with one false move he could have fallen to his death. Crawling back inside the booth, he sat in delight waiting for his cue. But when it came time to take the air, the cue never came. He looked through a thin panel separating him from Husing and saw Ted open right on the dot. Stern had cut his own NBC line by mistake.

Both Husing and Stern were in difficulty another time at the Vanderbilt-Alabama game in Nashville, Tennessee. Both booths were perched high above the rim of the stadium. When the announcers arrived, they found out that someone had painted both booths inside and out. The paint had not dried, which left the two announcers splotched with gray paint by the time the game ended. On the door to Husing's booth, painted in large letters, was a sign reading, "Ladies." On the door to Stern's booth was one word, "Men." The two network giants spent the entire afternoon trying to stay out of fresh paint and directing urgent and persistent ladies and gentlemen in other directions.

For several years Stern held a secret that few knew. The incompetent care given his leg after the auto accident led to his addiction to morphine and other pain-killing drugs. His career, meanwhile, was

Stern was an icon in sportscasting. *Courtesy of the author's collection*

flourishing. In 1940 he topped Ted Husing on the Radio Daily index, a position Ted had held for nine straight years. Stern held it amazingly for the next 13 years. Accolades and awards came his way as the nation's top sportscasting voice. He even appeared in a few motion pictures, including *Pride of the Yankees* with Gary Cooper. In 1951 he experienced one of his proudest moments when he won an Emmy Award.

Throughout those years, Bill was waging a losing battle with morphine and other prescription drugs. "There was an insecurity and emotional instability that

I didn't even know I had. I was in a business loaded with pressures. I knew I had to quit, and yet I enjoyed the effects of peace and calm that the drugs provided." Finally, in 1952 Bill entered a New England hospital with hopes of breaking his long and destructive drug habit, and after two weeks thought he had licked it. He soon learned, however, that 16 years of addiction are not erased in a few weeks, and after receiving news that he would not be assigned to the 1952 college football television schedule on NBC, an assignment he had drawn every year since 1937, he turned once again to narcotics. He was also demoted as sports director of NBC, replaced by Tom Gallery. Stern did do the games on radio, a blow to his pride, and he did the 1953 Cotton Bowl in Dallas before leaving NBC in the spring of 1953 to join ABC.

Finally, on the occasion of the 1956 Sugar Bowl, the bubble burst and it happened in front of a national TV audience. He arrived late for the broadcast, and his partner, Ray Scott, was preparing to do the game alone. In his book, *The Taste Of Ashes*, Stern recollected that day he hit bottom, a day after he had taken an overdose of dope plus an overdose of sleeping pills: "[I had started the broadcast,] 'This afternoon we bring you the Sugar Bowl classic between…' Between who? Then it came without a perceptible pause, 'Pittsburgh and Georgia Tech. Here are the starting lineups: For Pittsburgh at left end, Joe Walton…at left tackle Bob Pollock from Mt. Carmel, Pennsylvania. At left tackle…' No, I thought, I had said that, or had I? Slowly I started again. 'At left tackle, ah…' Bob who? Now where was his name? Here was a note. What did it say? I couldn't believe what it said. Why this was idiotic. Frowning, I read it again, but the words didn't

change. They still contained that short, terse order (from the network), 'Give it to Scott.' There was nothing to give to Ray Scott because he was already running with urgency through the list of players. What had I done!?!" ABC, searching for an excuse, announced that Stern had been involved in a car accident on the way to the stadium.

Bill Stern joined Mutual in 1957. *Photo courtesy of Westwood One*

Stern checked into Le Roy Hospital in New York to try once again to lick his addiction and was restrained from an attempt to kill himself by jumping through a window. He managed to do a 15-minute broadcast a day, but his voice was broken and scratchy. Letters came in accusing him of being drunk. A few months passed before Stern entered the Institute of Living Hospital in Hartford, Connecticut. He was there for six months, and the spontaneous concern from his vast audience brought a continuous flow of mail. "I never had one letter of condemnation, although I could have had plenty," Bill said. "These were all nice people who just sat down and took time to say, 'You've given us a lot of excitement and a lot of happiness. Now things aren't so easy for you, so we just want you to know we're thinking about you.'" The cravings, nerves, and nausea placed Bill one level below being declared legally insane. He wouldn't eat or sleep and was getting worse. The football season rolled by, and for the first time in 22 years he had missed broadcasting the opening game. "Here I sat, locked in the disturbed unit of a mental hospital. Bitterly, hopelessly, I knew the taste of ashes." Stern had finally hit bottom and was now ready to make a sincere effort to recover.

In February 1957, Stern launched his comeback as a disc jockey on WINS in New York and in August 1957 joined what he tabbed "the most fearless of the networks," Mutual. His old sponsor Colgate then showed their faith in him by sponsoring a biweekly morning sports show with Bill as host. It was an opinionated show that he was hoping NBC would broadcast, but to no avail. "There are too many sacred cows at NBC. You can't hit baseball because they broadcast the Game of the Week and the World Series.

You can't hit football because they broadcast college and pro football. You can't hit boxing because of the Gillette Cavalcade of Sports." ABC also passed on his show "after making me a bunch of promises, before getting scared." Stern then found a home on Mutual, and in 1958, had made it all the way back and was voted "Radio's Sportscaster of the Year" by *Radio & TV Daily*. It was also the comeback of the ages.

Like his predecessor, Graham McNamee, Stern was never a stickler for accuracy. He was much more interested in drama and excitement and the entertainment value that sports provided. That is why his *Colgate Sports Newsreel Show* was so important to him. It mirrored the show business personality that meant so much to him. Sports was just the vehicle that he tapped into for most of his story lines.

Bill Stern's Colgate Sports Newsreel Show made its debut in October 1939. Babe Ruth was his first guest. Searching for a new twist that would appeal to everyone and not just sports fans, Stern talked about some of the great names in history and gave them a sports connection. Stern spun yarns so implausible that only the most gullible could believe them. Each program opened with a dramatic story, followed with a guest interview, and would close with another melodramatic vignette. The stories were set to music and fableized and dramatized so they would appeal to the housewife as well as her sports-hungry husband. The show was a smash from the start, but the press ridiculed it something fierce. "I've got news for the press," Stern said toward the end of his career. "I laughed all the way to the bank. By far, it was the most popular sports program ever on radio. Why should I change a winning format because of mockery and derision? The show was strictly for entertainment, and we, therefore, took dramatic license and liberties with the stories. The press couldn't see this. They regarded the program as strictly of a sports nature, and I never did. In fact, I wanted to take the sports out of it completely. In a way similar to the movies, which take the highlights and skip the day-to-day boredom of life, I built my script. I might start at the end of a man's life, cut to the beginning, and then the middle. 'This isn't sports reporting,' shouted the press. Before we took the air, I had investigated and found no sports show had ever lasted more than a year on the network. Our stories on people were beautifully written, and frankly I didn't care what the critics thought. I didn't like them, and they sure didn't care much for me. Newspapermen were basically jealous of radio men because broadcasters made 10 times as much money as they did, and they felt the announcers didn't know as much about sports as they did, which is probably true." When he started the Colgate show, he was making $75 a week. As the years went by he was making as much as $2,500 a week.

"I've got news for the press, I laughed all the way to the bank. By far, it was the most popular sports program ever on radio. Why should I change a winning format because of mockery and derision? The show was strictly for entertainment, and we, therefore, took dramatic license and liberties with the stories." —Bill Stern

Famous names provided the impetus for Bill's Colgate show: "Brash, irrepressible Leo Durocher with his raucous amiability; tennis ace Bill Tilden, who considered himself a magnificent Shakespearean actor but actually was quite hammy; Lucille Ball and her infectious sense of humor; Jack Benny with his unequalled sense of timing, which turned a funny line into a sidesplitting one; the ear-soothing Andrews sisters; reserved and aloof Bobby Jones; boisterous, back-slapping Jack Dempsey, always the champion; The Lone Ranger, complete with mask and six guns to get me in the proper mood; Pat O'Brien, filming Knute Rockne of Notre Dame and living the role even off the set; and bashful, lanky, Jimmy Stewart, a great Princeton rooter and the most modest man I've ever known." Stern had a great team of writers on the show. Among them Mike Cowles, who later published *Look* magazine; Charlie Peck, who later wrote a Broadway musical that starred Maureen O'Hara; Alfred Palka, who produced several movies; Bill Davidson, a former *Look* associate editor; Barney Nagler, a great boxing and horse racing scribe; and recognized columnist Mac Davis. The talent fees for one show amounted to $4,300 with every word scored and set to original music by a full orchestra.

Television forced the demise of the *Sports Newsreel* in 1951 after a 12-year run. "Bill had a wild imagination," longtime New York baseball writer Fred Lieb remembered. "I never listened to him after one show in which he told of a girl who had played two weeks with the Giants under John McGraw without anyone knowing it." Wrote *Atlanta Journal* columnist Ed Danforth in his column, "An Ear to the Ground": "This department would no more undertake to correct one of Bill Stern's sports broadcasts than it would to try to straighten out Al Capp on details of an adventure of Lil' Abner. Both features are creations of artists in fiction. He deals in the dramatic episodes and brings to the microphone notable histrionic talents. Only envious rivals say he hams it up. Stern is courageous. Where the dull facts of an incident lack warmth, Bill supplies the deficiency. Other commentators cravenly follow the fetish of accuracy and are as dull as record books. Bill sifts the facts, discarding tasteless details and substituting pure fancy."

Stern figured in two historic television sports firsts. On May 17, 1939, he announced the first televised sports event in history as Columbia hosted Princeton in baseball at Baker Field. NBC telecast the game with one camera as Princeton won 2-1 in 10 innings. Later that same year, Stern also telecast the first college football game, Fordham versus Waynesburg on September 30, 1939, on the experimental W2XBS. The Rams beat Waynesburg handily 34-7.

Harry Wismer's sportscasting experience would be invaluable to football as a million-dollar enterprise. *Photo courtesy of News Talk 1290 WHIO Radio in Dayton, Ohio*

(Three weeks later, on October 22, 1939, the first professional football game was televised from Ebbets Field in Brooklyn. NBC's flagship, W2XBS, carried the pictures of the Dodgers' 23-14 win over Philadelphia in a game attended by 13,051 fans. There was no mention of the first NFL telecast in the next day's *New York Times*. Only 500 TV sets received the broadcast. Allen "Skip" Walz described the game. There were no monitors, no spotters, and no visual aids. A workforce of eight people put the game on the air. Walz remembers the two quarterbacks. "Ace Parker quarterbacked the Dodgers and Davey O'Brien the Eagles, but the difference was Ralph Kercheval's three field goals.")

Although Stern basked in the trappings of being a national celebrity, he said he would have done something else if he had it to do over again. "I made more money than I could have in another walk of life, but I wouldn't submit myself to the pressures in broadcasting if I could do it again. I haven't faced a microphone yet where I haven't had butterflies in my stomach."

Stern spent his last several years in broadcasting doing sports for the Mutual network. He died of a heart attack at his Rye, New York, home on November 19, 1971. He was 64 years old.

Both Stern and Ted Husing displayed enormous egos, but both would have to step aside for Harry Wismer when it came to ego and self-idolatry. Wismer was in a class by himself. As a broadcaster, self-promoter, league founder, and league failure, Wismer cut a boisterous swath through American sports in the 1940s, 1950s, and well into the 1960s, before it all came crashing down. Husing was tops at CBS, Stern was the lynchpin at NBC, and Wismer was the sports headliner on ABC. Braggadocio was Harry's middle name. First as an errand boy, then as a broadcaster, and finally as part

Wismer during his years as the owner of the AFL's New York Titans. *Photo provided by AP/WWP*

owner of the Detroit Lions and the Washington Redskins, football was his business. In his book, *The Public Calls It Sport*, Wismer summed up his philosophy. "I have always been a hustler, and I'm proud of it. No one ever gave me anything. What I made I made through my own efforts. I broke some rules, trod on some toes, gambled, and risked. I thought I had all the answers. I hadn't learned that no matter how good you think you are, how shrewd you are, there is always someone down the block, across the street, in the next town, who is a little better, shrewder, more ruthless." That man turned out to be William Shea, who let Harry's dreams die at the ramshackle Polo Grounds with Sonny Werblin providing the final punch by watching Wismer go broke and then reaping the riches of Shea Stadium as the new owner of the Titans-turned-Jets.

Wismer watches his team beat the Denver Broncos on Thanksgiving Day. Wismer negotiated the television rights to AFL games. *Photo provided by AP/WWP*

By the time I first met up with Wismer, he had dropped from the scene with numerous physical problems that had seen him bounce from hospital to hospital with a grave illness. From the Mayo Clinic to his hometown hospital in Port Huron, Michigan, Harry had been laid up for over seven months. His voice on the phone in the summer of 1967 seemed hollow. He lacked enthusiasm, sounding depressed and deflated. He had a right to be, after a disastrous tenure as owner of the ill-fated New York Titans of the American Football League had left him broke and broken. Then there was the Michigan Speedway project that was stagnating. Then his collapse after an overseas trip and subsequent hospitalization.

I was amazed at how well he looked when I arrived at the hospital. Through all the anguish of the months in hospitals battling cancer, having a cancerous hip replaced, and other maladies, he looked prosperous, as only he could look after everything had been pulled out from under him. "I've been under wraps for too long," he muttered. "I'm anxious to get out of here and get going again."

Tracks 15-16

The physical problems had begun years earlier when he was in the midst of the Titan disaster. He ignored his condition because he was too busy trying to pay his bills and keep the franchise afloat. He only dealt with it after he had sold the franchise to Sonny Werblin, giving birth to the Jets. Shea Stadium followed, a far cry from the dilapidated Polo Grounds that his Titans were forced to play in.

The months of seclusion in five different hospitals had afforded Wismer time to think, to contemplate, and to take stock over friends lost, a wrecked marriage, and financial failings. "It all seems so long ago," he sighed when thinking back to his glory days. "The broadcast days, running football teams, it all seems like a dream."

Tranquility had not been part of the Wismer persona. His feuds had been many and storied. He had a career-long disagreement with his former employer, George Preston Marshall of the Washington Redskins. Disenchantment also existed between Harry and Lamar Hunt. The two were cofounders of the American Football League, although Hunt gets most of the credit and even has a Hall of Fame bust in Canton. But it was Wismer who negotiated the lucrative two-million dollar TV contract with ABC that kept the league afloat in the first few seasons. He also feuded with the AFL's first commissioner, Joe Foss, and his Titan coach, the legendary Sammy Baugh. When your team is drawing just 114,682 paid admissions, like the Titans did in their inaugural 1960 season, you have to blame somebody. By 1962 the Titans were drawing only 36,161 for the entire season.

Deserted by the world he thought he owned and abandoned by those he thought were his friends, this pathetic, wheelchair-bound man of 53 was a far cry from the broadcaster who enthralled millions of listeners and kept them on the edges of their seats. Accuracy might not have been Harry's forte, but nobody ever flicked off the radio because of boredom when he was calling the shots.

Wismer, born in 1915 and raised in Port Huron, spent 30 years in sportscasting. An all-around athlete himself who earned letters in football, basketball, and baseball, along with being an avid tennis player, Harry idolized Detroit announcer Ty Tyson. After graduating from St. John's Military Academy in Delafield, Wisconsin, where he played football and basketball and was awarded Athlete of the Year honors, Wismer hitchhiked to Florida where he played for Charlie Bachman at the University of Florida. When Bachman was named head coach at Michigan State, succeeding his old Notre Dame teammate Jimmy Crowley, he brought Harry north with him as an office assistant and personal secretary. "I was a 175-pound quarterback with the Spartans and also did the punting," Wismer said. He also served as sports editor of the *Michigan State News*. His football career ended when he blew out his knee against Michigan.

With Bachman's help, Wismer hooked on with a campus radio station where he began broadcasting sports. Then, in 1934, Wismer accompanied Bachman down to Detroit to watch a Lions game against the Philadelphia Yellowjackets. Bachman was a guest of Dick Richards, who owned the Lions and radio station WJR. During the game, Richards turned to Bachman and said, "I wish I could get somebody decent to handle the P.A. system for me. The guy doing it now is driving me nuts. I feel like I'm at a wake." Bach

115

suggested Richards give Harry a shot, and he was hired for $10 a game. Richards also gave him a job on WJR covering professional football with the title Lions Cub Reporter.

Because Richards had never heard Harry on radio, it was a bit of a gamble, but the following week he did the P.A. as the Lions hosted Ernie Nevers and the Chicago Cardinals, which ended in a 20-20 tie. "More importantly, Richards liked my performance and I ended up doing a daily 10-minute radio show each night on WJR."

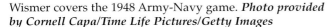

Wismer covers the 1948 Army-Navy game. *Photo provided by Cornell Capa/Time Life Pictures/Getty Images*

Harry was still attending school in East Lansing at the time, so each day he hitchhiked the 75 miles each way and did so for two years. "Many of the people who picked me up recognized my name from the radio as I was getting more and more exposure on the air," Harry said.

After the 1936 season, Bachman encouraged Harry to quit school and take over the sports directorship of WJR. Bachman was convinced that Harry had a future in radio. He felt ambition and experience were more important than an education. So Harry left Michigan State with just two semesters left until graduation. "Things were different then," Harry added. "A college degree didn't mean as much. Bachman would be run out of town if he told a kid today to quit school and start working."

In 1941 Wismer was hired by NBC as sports director of the Blue network, the forerunner of ABC, replacing the legendary Graham McNamee and working with Bill Stern. Both Ted Husing and Stern encouraged Harry not to dip below their rate for doing a game. "Don't worry, you've got nothing to worry about," Harry replied. "My rate is $2,500." They laughed, but Harry wasn't kidding, and soon the more established members of the Big Three had raised their rate to match his.

After broadcasting some of the top events in sports, from football to golf, the network made a costly decision, abandoning sports under new ABC president Robert Kintner, who did not believe in athletics taking up valuable broadcast time on radio. "We lost the College All-Star Game, the Masters, the Sugar Bowl, and the baseball All-Star Game, among many other events," Harry said, grimacing. "It was a disaster, and after joining NBC, he did the same thing, costing the networks millions of dollars in advertising revenue."

Harry loved broadcasting sports. "More than any man could ever love anything," he stressed. "I looked forward to every trip and every event." The first college football game Wismer ever broadcast took place in Lafayette, Indiana, at Purdue's Ross-Ade Stadium and went coast to coast. Soon he was doing network college football on a weekly basis. "They used to call Husing, Stern, and me the 'Big Three' because we handled the bulk of the nation's sports broadcasting. Each network would bid on a Monday for the college football games coming up that week. The three of us sat and worked out who was going to do what so that no duplication would occur." Long-term contracts and rights fees were still unheard of in the early 1940s. "In a typical week, I might be in Athens, Georgia, for the Georgia-Georgia Tech game; Stern would fly to Los Angeles to broadcast Southern Cal, while Husing journeyed to South Bend to broadcast the Irish." Wismer referred to Husing as "an odd sort of fellow. I always admired his work and no one can doubt that he was one of the finest broadcasters who ever lived. I tried to combine the styles of Husing, who had a great voice and strived for accuracy, and Stern, who thought drama was more important than who was carrying the ball."

Wismer became known for his dropping of famous names and close associates whom he would announce as being in the crowd. Dwight Eisenhower, John F. Kennedy, J. Edgar Hoover, Harry Truman, and Joan Crawford were just some names he would announce as being in attendance, even though they might be hundreds of miles away. "I worked with Harry Wismer quite often," veteran announcer Jim Britt recalled. "He was a real fan, one of the most enthusiastic men I have ever met. Harry was all things; salesman, promoter, broadcaster. Trouble is, he never figured out which he was most suited for. Harry was a namedropper, and his broadcasts of long touchdown runs were the lengthiest ever recorded. By the time the runner meandered his way from one end of the field to the other, Harry had plotted his course is such a way that the running back ran past some of the biggest names in politics and show business."

Harry's long association as the voice of the Washington Redskins got its start in 1941 when he sold the American Oil Company on the rising popularity of pro football. Harry expanded the coverage area to include several states as he built the Redskins network. For 15 seasons Harry aired Redskins games, beginning with the 73-0 championship game in 1940 in which the Bears pulverized the Redskins. "It was a rout from Bill Osmanski's opening touchdown run to the 19-point fourth quarter. The Bears had compassion for the Redskins in the second quarter, only scoring a touchdown. It was a shattering experience to say the least." Wismer's interest in the Redskins didn't confine itself to the broadcast booth. Owner George Preston Marshall sold Harry six shares of stock in the club in 1947 and added 14 more shares later, totaling $35,000 or 25 percent of the ball club. Harry became a director and vice president of the Redskins, reporting only to Marshall. By the mid- to late 1950s, Wismer and Marshall were feuding over a number of issues, including Marshall's refusal to sign African-American players. Harry sued Marshall for half a million dollars, and when he sold his stock, Marshall worked hard to

Wismer (above left) and Lamar Hunt helped found the American Football Leauge; (below) Coach Sammy Baugh (left) and Wismer pose with the Titans schedule. *Photos courtesy of the author's collection*

1960 HOME SCHEDULE TITANS OF NEW YORK at the POLO GROUNDS

SEPT. 11 BUFFALO SUN.
16 BOSTON FRI. NITE
23 DENVER FRI. NITE
OCT. 23 HOUSTON SUN.
28 OAKLAND FRI. NITE
NOV. 4 LOS ANGELES FRI. NITE
NOV. 24 DALLAS THANKSGIVING DAY

Shepherd, Glenn Presnell, and Dutch Clark were just a sampling." Harry, with the backing of owner Dick Richards, secured General Mills, the makers of Wheaties, as a chief sponsor of Lions games. "The Breakfast of Champions" soon became the top sponsor of the league, thanks to the farsighted thinking of young Wismer, who was learning the innerworkings of a pro football franchise.

Beginning in the mid-1950s Wismer also broadcast Notre Dame football for many years. "I sold the advertising to Pontiac and presented the idea to Athletic Director Moose Krause and University President Father Hesburgh. Since that time, the Notre Dame network on Mutual has become the largest in the country."

Wismer was proud of his record as a sportscaster, saying it was unchallenged by anyone. "In a 20-year period I broadcast more sporting events than all the other network guys put together. I traveled over seven million miles by air in the process and lived like a gypsy. I never got over the thrill of sitting behind a microphone."

He couldn't say the same for the business side of sports. He retired from broadcasting to sink his time and money into the New York entry in the AFL. His selling of the TV contract for $1,785,000 gave the league early exposure and legitimacy. It was called the Wismer Plan, with the proceeds divided equally among the member teams. It was new to pro football, with the NFL adopting the concept later. "We didn't have an established league," Harry said. "We had to launch one. Everybody had to get some money, or one or two

try to destroy Harry's top announcing contracts. In some instances he succeeded. "I sold my Redskin stock in 1962 to cover bills with the Titans, and it had grown in value to $350,000. That stock would have mushroomed to two million dollars just five years later if I'd have held on."

Before joining the Redskins, Wismer also had an interest in the Detroit Lions, both as a broadcaster from 1935 to 1941 and as a stockholder. "The Lions were loaded with talent in those days," Wismer remembered. "Buddy Parker, Ace Gutowski, Bill clubs would prosper for a time and then the league would fail." Lamar Hunt, Harry said, was jealous of his expertise and was a "babe in arms" compared to my consultants, George Halas and George Preston Marshall. "Hunt bought his way into football, has little knowledge of the game, and time will prove it," Wismer said. Harry was also responsible for Buffalo getting the Bills, for Boston getting the Patriots, and for helping the Chargers settle in Los Angeles with Barron Hilton. One of the last articles written about him was written by Joe Falls of the *Detroit Free Press* in 1966 in which Harry predicted an NFL-AFL merger, with Pete Rozelle emerging as sole commissioner of pro football. "Rozelle has the flexibility, the personality and the charm to handle the job," Wismer said. "He's not vicious and he's not a crook." About Wismer, Falls wrote: "He can turn on the charm, click, and turn off the charm, click, stepping nimbly from one movie camera to the next and not mix a metaphor along the way, somehow managing to use the perpendicular pronoun 'I' at least once a minute," Falls wrote.

"There's nothing bashful about Harry Baby," said one critic. "They didn't split Gaul into three parts—he's got it all."

Coaching the first edition of the Titans was one of the true legends of the sport, Sammy Baugh, who Harry knew from his days in Washington. "Baugh had some great qualities. He was a winner, which was why I picked him as coach. Sammy laid a solid foundation the first two years. We were 7-7 the first year, but the combination of the lousy stadium and the Giants' TV saturation did us in. The other franchises fared better, because they were situated in noncompetitive regions." There was also a contingent of New York sports

writers, led by Harold Weisman and Dan Parker, who did everything to run Harry out of business.

Wismer lost more than his shirt in New York. Two and a half million dollars to be exact. "The biggest reason I lost the two and a half million was the new stadium wasn't completed in time. My four-year-old grandson could make money in Shea Stadium. We were forced to play in the antiquated old Polo Grounds, which offered no comfort to the spectator." To his credit, Wismer avoided bankruptcy, paying off 78 cents on every dollar. When Harry needed help the most, his fellow owners, Hunt, Bill Shea, and Bud Adams, all turned their backs on him.

Which brings us to 1967 and Harry's physical battles. The last of the Big-Time Operators was lonely and depressed. After so many operations, he wondered if he was doomed. At first, the odds of his survival were 80 to 20 against. He beat the odds and was gearing for a return to broadcasting. "I'll only begin to live again when I return to New York City. I've been walking more and more every day," he added as I wheeled him down the corridor before saying goodbye. "This weekend I hope to walk around the block with just a pair of crutches to help me." As I departed, I formed a mental picture of the man as he leaned against a metal railing, gripping it for support.

That was the last contact I had with Harry Wismer. In the months that followed, his condition improved dramatically. His dream of returning to New York came to fruition, but rather than being welcomed by open arms, he was, for the most part, ignored. Enemies outnumbered friends. Seeking solace, he began drinking heavily, and on the night of December 2, 1967, just four months after our get-together in Port Huron, he went on a binge and suffered a fatal fall down a flight of stairs in a New York restaurant. The former announcing great died the following morning. He was just 53 years old. The autopsy indicated a fractured skull as the cause of death.

The last of the Big-Time Operators was denied the chance to go out on top, denied the chance to regain his lost fortune and personal respectability. A broken heart might have been the real cause of death.

Harry Wismer was a visionary. In the early 1950s he realized the impact that television was going to make on the sport. In 1951 he arranged for the first telecast of the Pro Bowl from the Los Angeles Coliseum. He, of course, was the broadcaster. He saw right away how football was meant for television because of its back-and-forth nature and hard-hitting contact. The development of slow-motion replays only added to the appeal.

The emergence of regionalized coverage of games at the expense of nationwide broadcasts created opportunities for several broadcasters to become intertwined with pro football. Although Wismer's

Television turned America's love of football into an obsession and a lucrative business. Curt Gowdy stands behind the camera to check the shot. *Photo courtesy of Curt Gowdy*

league, the AFL, featured the announcing pair of Curt Gowdy and Paul Christman on a nationwide scope every Sunday on ABC, the NFL on CBS, by the mid-1950s, had a sportscaster in every city. It was the same face on every game in each home area, which deeply identified the broadcaster and the team. In New York, Chris Schenkel was the voice of the Giants, describing the action of Y.A. Tittle, Frank Gifford, Sam Huff, and company. Deliberate and dramatic, Ray Scott was the voice of Vince Lombardi's Green Bay Packers. When Johnny Unitas faded back to pass in Baltimore, Chuck Thompson was calling the plays to the rabid Colts faithful. When Jimmy Brown reeled off another 80-yard

Waynesburg and Fordham face off in football's first televised game on September 30, 1939. *Photo courtesy of NBC*

run for the Cleveland Browns, Ken Coleman was with him stride for stride. Jack Whitaker was the voice of the Eagles in Philadelphia; Jim Gibbons did the honors in Washington with the Redskins; Gil Stratton in Los Angeles with "Crazy Legs" Hirsch and Norm Van Brocklin; Bob Fouts and Lon Simmons with the 49ers in San Francisco; Van Patrick became as identifiable in Detroit as Bobby Layne and Yale Lary; Jack Drees was in St. Louis with the Cardinals and Frank Gleiber in Dallas with the Cowboys. Jack Brickhouse worked with former Bear George Conner in Chicago. Other former players who became color analysts were Warren Lahr in Cleveland, Pat Summerall in New York, and Don Paul in Los Angeles. In the mid-1960s, Tom Harmon anchored a Saturday pregame show called *Countdown to Kickoff* that went from city to city setting up the next day's games.

The AFL, with the team of Curt Gowdy and Paul Christman, was a league geared for television. Players such as Lance Alworth, Charlie Tolar, Billy Cannon, and George Blanda became familiar all over the country on the AFL broadcasts. Gate receipts weren't paying the freight, TV receipts were. Finally, the merger brought the playing field onto a common standing where it was one for all and all for one. And football's popularity made it a rival for America's greatest past-time, baseball. The gridiron became a battlefield for television and radio to grab viewers and listeners. Football broadcasting became a big business, and football became part of the American consciousness.

The Golden Roll Call

Joe Boland

Of all the ex-players who have gravitated into football broadcasting, Joe Boland might have been the very first. As a stout, strong lineman at Notre Dame under Coach Knute Rockne, Boland was a massive 216 pounds, quite a big man in those days, and he helped open holes for the legendary Four Horsemen. His defensive performance against Stanford and Ernie Nevers on New Year's Day in 1925 helped the Irish to a 27-10 win and a national championship. One of six brothers, the Philadelphia native grew up wanting to play for the Irish. When he broke his leg in a collision with boyhood pal and teammate Joe Maxwell in October 1926 in a 20-7 win against the University of Minnesota, his career was suddenly over.

After graduating in 1927, Joe took a coaching job as a line coach under Adam Walsh at Santa Clara. Then, aided by Rockne's influence, came the head coaching job at St. Thomas College in St. Paul. When St. Thomas, strapped for money during the Depression, cut his salary in half, Joe took his first job in radio. It was at WCCO in Minneapolis. His audition consisted of making up and broadcasting an imaginary game, which he did with flying colors. In 1933 he broadcast Minnesota football during the exciting Bernie Bierman era. Then, in 1934, came a call from new Irish coach Elmer Layden to return to South Bend as line coach, which out of duty to the school of Our Lady, he accepted. His salary was $3,000, less than he would have made if he stayed at St. Thomas. Seven years later, Layden became commissioner of the National Football League, and Joe was once again looking for gainful employment. After one more year in coaching as a Purdue assistant, Joe decided to devote his

Joe Boland as a player. *Photo courtesy of Notre Dame Sports Information Department*

attention to radio and returned in 1941 to South Bend where he began broadcasting Notre Dame football.

After one season, WGN in Chicago offered Joe a job, but the hours were awful. He returned to South Bend to broadcast the Irish, freelancing as voice of the Chicago Cardinals during their championship 1948 season and for several years thereafter. Warren Brown wrote, "He knew his subjects. His listeners, who were countless, knew they could depend on him. The team

Track 38

Boland (left) as a Notre Dame line coach in 1937. Boland put together Notre Dame's radio network. *Photos courtesy of Notre Dame Sports Information Department*

of Joe Boland and Paul Christman established a level that perhaps will never be attained."

In South Bend, Boland helped put together the Notre Dame Network, which continues on Westwood One radio today. The original nucleus was put together by Joe in 1947, and by 1951, 40 stations had come aboard. By 1955 the number had grown to 190 stations. Armed Forces Radio also began carrying the Irish games. "In point of fact, Joe Boland was the Irish Football Network," said Franklin Schurz, publisher of the *South Bend Tribune*. "He conceived it. He planned and organized it. He worked out the hundreds of painstaking technical details that made it possible. Then he went on the air, and hundreds of thousands of fans around the globe went on the air with him."

Notre Dame's national appeal, coupled with its subway alumni, created a huge listening audience, and

Joe Boland had no rival in painting the word picture. "He was one of the first to combine great technical knowledge of football with the other attributes it takes to make an announcer," former Notre Dame Sports Information Director Joe Petritz said. "A colorful vocabulary; a pleasing natural voice; and a rapid-fire delivery, which sometimes pleased by just barely failing to keep pace with his swift mind."

By its last season in 1955, the Irish Network competed on the same level as the national networks.

Boland (above, left) interviews Minnesota coach Clarence "Doc" Spears and Knute Rockne in 1929; Boland (below, center) talks to Irish All-Americans Bob Williams (left) and Jerry Groom. *Photos courtesy of Notre Dame Sports Information Department*

The Notre Dame hierarchy sold the rights to Mutual before the 1956 season, and they've remained on Mutual/Westwood One ever since with announcers such as Van Patrick, Al Wester, Don Criqui, and Tony Roberts following Joe Boland. Roberts will celebrate his 25th season as the voice of the Irish in 2004.

A stickler for pregame preparation, Boland spent the year amassing information on teams he was broadcasting. During the season he would fall asleep at night memorizing names and numbers. "Accuracy was a fetish with Joe," wrote his wife, Peg, in her book, *Joe Boland, Notre Dame Man.* "There was no compromise with the truth. He felt that careless reporting was an insult to his listeners, unfair to the men playing the game." Joe Boland

broadcast a football game, "the way Joe DiMaggio played center field," was the way one writer summed it up. "In a profession that is liberally sprinkled with hypocrites and schemers, Joe never soiled himself or his name," said Jim Butz, a longtime friend.

In 1959 Boland was still keeping up a furious pace of working at the radio station, broadcasting Irish football, and telecasting Cardinal football on Sundays. After the bowl season, the Boland's headed east to New York for a vacation and big family reunion in Philadelphia. Then in February came the Indiana state basketball tourney, which Joe broadcast wall to wall. On the night of February 25, 1960, exhausted from broadcasting three basketball games in one day, Joe fell

asleep reading a book and suddenly at 4:00 a.m., Peg heard "terrible, frightening sounds. I jumped out of bed and turned on the light. The police came quickly, despite the heavy snowdrifts, but there was nothing they could do. Joe was gone, without ever knowing what struck him." Like his mentor, Knute Rockne, Joe Boland left this world all too young, dying of a heart attack. He was only 55 years old. His funeral in South Bend rivaled the size of Rockne's.

Dick Bray

Dick Bray was a rarity. He was one of the few men who became a top-flight referee and a respected play-by-play broadcaster. He was a master of the rules on the field and adept enough in the booth to report with logic and understanding. The youngest to referee in the Big Ten, Dick was a respected baseball, football, and basketball announcer around his hometown Cincinnati area for more than 30 years.

Bing Crosby stops by to chat with Boland during halftime of the Notre Dame-Southern California game. *Photo courtesy of Notre Dame Sports Information Department*

Dick played quarterback in a backup role at Xavier University and started to referee CYO games for $2.50 a game. He moved up the ladder quickly and in his early twenties was refereeing college football and basketball, teaming often with Frank Lane, who would later serve as general manager of several major league baseball teams. "I was a midget next to Frank," Dick said. "He'd roll his sleeves up, and his arms would bulge like a blacksmith's."

In 1934 Dick broke into radio on WKRC at age 33. He broadcast Reds baseball, and in 1937 teamed with Red Barber on station

through the open end of the stadium, I was bursting with so much pride I almost had to stop my broadcast." Dick is the only man ever to both officiate and broadcast a game of the stature of Notre Dame-Navy.

A stickler for perfection, Dick would send copies of his game broadcasts to Ted Husing who would listen to them, make corrections, and send them back. For 10 years he combined the duties of refereeing and announcing before concentrating solely on radio in 1945. "I didn't want to serve two masters," he said. "I didn't feel it was right to go to Notre Dame in the fall to announce football and then come back in the winter

Left: Dick Bray with his mike pack in 1940. Below: Bray behind the mike for WHIO. *Left photo courtesy of 1530 WSAI; Right photo courtesy of News Talk 1290 WHIO in Dayton, Ohio*

WSAI. Dick's greatest claim to fame was his *Fans in the Stands* program heard before every Reds game where he interviewed fans, ushers, groundskeepers, vendors, and players.

Dick's biggest thrill occurred when he broadcast a Navy-Notre Dame game in Baltimore. "I had never seen the Midshipmen march on, and while I was down on the field doing my pregame interview, I heard this clomp, clomp, clomp sound behind me. I turned and there was the Brigade, whom I was told wasn't coming as the war was going on. When I saw those boys come to referee basketball. I felt I could go further in broadcasting. My last game was between Notre Dame and Marquette in basketball, and afterward I tossed my whistle out into the snow under the Golden Dome of Our Lady."

Dick Bray passed away in 1986 at age 83.

Jack Buck

Besides his great career as a baseball broadcaster, Jack Buck was equally adept as a football announcer. In fact his football broadcasting career spanned more than 50 years, from his days announcing Ohio State football to his later years teaming with Hank Stram on NFL football on CBS Radio.

As a teenager and a young adult, broadcasting was just a distant dream. He grew up in Holyoke, Massachusetts, and moved to Cleveland as a teenager. His love of athletics probably came from his father. "My dad worked for the Erie railroad and was one of the best athletes that Holyoke High ever produced," Jack said. "He pitched a perfect game while in high school, retiring 27 men in a row, and when he didn't pitch, he played first base and batted fourth. He had a tryout with the Giants, but he and John McGraw began arguing about something and Dad walked away."

In high school, Jack worked four jobs and still went to school. "In the morning I awoke to deliver a shopping paper that hung on doorknobs. After school I worked in an ice cream factory, sold the *Cleveland Press* on a street corner, and then headed to a drive-in restaurant where I would work sometimes until three in the morning." That work ethic set the pattern of his life.

Jack's life was fraught with peril, working on the ore boats of the Great Lakes as a 17-year-old just out of

high school to serving as an army infantryman in World War II, seeing action on the front lines in Germany and helping to capture the Remagen Bridge before the Germans could blow it up, thus seizing one of Hitler's last natural strongholds. Wounded in the left arm, Jack was released on VE Day in May 1945.

Taking advantage of the G.I. Bill upon his return to the states, Jack enrolled at Ohio State, where, two years later, he launched his broadcast career on the campus station, WOSU. He split the sportscasting duties with a student named Dick Bull, teaming up on *The Buck and Bull Show*. Soon after he joined commercial station WCOL, where he was paid five dollars a broadcast. He had told the station he had worked on Armed Forces Radio during the war. "It was one of the many tactical lies I've told in my life," Jack laughed. "I'm a pretty good liar. In this business you get to be after awhile."

The first event Jack ever broadcast was an Ohio State-DePaul basketball game. He knew the Buckeye team well because he was one of the last cuts by Coach Tippy Dye. Afterward his professor told him to find something else to do for a living. Fortunately he didn't, and in a matter of months he was doing Columbus Red Bird baseball and Ohio State football. "Wes Fesler was in his last year as coach when I began doing their games," Jack said. "Ohio State was known as the 'Graveyard of Coaches' at that time, and when Wes stepped down, I campaigned for Woody Hayes, who became the most successful coach in Buckeye annals." Vic Janowicz was running and passing his way to the Heisman Trophy in 1950, and Buck was behind the microphone. One of the memorable games he did was the famed 1950 "Blizzard Bowl" against Michigan, played in a raging snowstorm. "It was Homecoming,

The voices of the American Football League in the 1960s—George Ratterman, Paul Christman, Jack Buck, and Curt Gowdy. *Photo courtesy of Curt Gowdy*

and over 82,000 tickets had been sold. By daylight on Saturday a foot of snow was on the ground and the wind was howling," cringed Jack at the memory of it. "By game time, conditions were unbearable. Only a few brave thousands made their way into the Horseshoe. Passing was impossible, and the running backs couldn't cut. Somehow Janowicz kicked a 35-yard field goal into the wind and snow that gave Ohio State a 3-2 lead after the first quarter. Then Michigan, behind quarterback Chuck Ortmann, blocked a Janowicz punt late in the second period, scored a touchdown, and went to the Rose Bowl even though they failed to make a first down all afternoon. There were, all together, 45 punts in the game. Spotting boards were useless because you couldn't see who had the ball or what yard line you were on. Over four inches of snow fell during the game alone. It was strictly guesswork. I remember opening the windows to try and see better and all the snow came pouring in. I couldn't see the sideline markers or the yard markers. That was one of the most challenging broadcasts I was ever involved in, up until the 20-below-zero game in Green Bay on the last day of December 1967."

In 1952 Jack joined WBNS-TV in Columbus to do a sports show and a morning variety show. One of his coworkers was a talented young comedian from Dayton, Ohio, named Jonathan Winters. "I was Jonathan's adviser," Jack remembered. "I used to feed him topics to extemporize around on his nightly comedy show."

Jack wasn't at WBNS long, because he became the voice of the Rochester Red Wings and then in 1954 he joined Harry Caray in the St. Louis Cardinals broadcast booth. A year doing the baseball *Game of the Week* on

ABC-TV helped Jack land a prime post along with Curt Gowdy of broadcasting the infant American Football League in 1960. "I announced one of the first games the AFL ever played, the Oakland Raiders versus the Los Angeles Chargers. Eddie Erdelatz and Sid Gillman were the respective coaches, and the final score was typical of the wide-open AFL, 52-28 Los Angeles."

In the three years Jack did AFL football, he watched the league, the cities, and the owners develop. "I was on the field holding the microphone when Houston and Dallas went into sudden death at Houston's Jeppessen Stadium on December 23, 1962. Abner Haynes represented the Texans when the coin was tossed and was a bit groggy from a blow to the head near the end of regulation. To everyone's disbelief, he said, 'We'll kick to the clock,' which meant he was giving Houston the ball and kicking into a 30-mph wind at the same time. I thought Dallas coach Hank Stram was going to keel over on the spot. That was one instance where I didn't know what to do. I was holding the mike up to Haynes's mouth, and since I knew Abner, I darn near blurted, 'Abner, that isn't what you want to do!' But I held back." Fortunately for Dallas, the Texans won 20-17 on rookie Tommy Brooker's 25-yard field goal almost 18 minutes into sudden death. "Stram had given Abner instructions that if he lost the toss, to take the clock and kick off with the wind. But he got mixed up on two counts and gave Houston the ball and kicked into the wind at the same time."

At 7:30 a.m. on the day the Dallas Cowboys met the Green Bay Packers in Green Bay for the NFL championship in 1967, the hotel operator woke Jack on the phone, saying, "Good morning Mr. Buck. It's 7:30, and it's 20 degrees below zero." "Usually when the operator wakes me, I put the phone down and doze a bit longer, but when she told me how cold it was outside, I was jolted into reality. By the time I got to Lambeau Field at 10:30, it had started to warm up, to 17 below. By game time it was 15 below, and I was out of business. Never in my life have I been that cold. Ray Scott did the first half and I did the second, making some mistakes because I couldn't think or concentrate properly. Frank Gifford and I got a little mixed up on the down when Dallas was staging their goal-line stand, and I wasn't too proud of my performance in that game. Survival took precedence over accuracy."

After the game, Buck, Gifford, and Tom Brookshire flew in a private plane from Green Bay to Chicago. After they took off one of the doors flew open. "If you thought it was cold on the field in Green Bay, you should have been up about 2,000 feet," remembered Jack, shivering at the thought. "Gifford tried to slam the door shut, but the arm rest came off after he yanked on it, making it impossible to close. It stayed open the entire trip with Giff holding the door trying to keep it from swinging open. We landed on an icy airstrip in Wisconsin, and when we finally got to Chicago, I celebrated New Year's Eve with the hottest bath I've ever had in my life."

Buck broadcast Dallas Cowboy football in the mid- to late 1960s and lived and died with the Cowboys. "I was involved to the point where I'd like to have died when a Dallas lineman pulled out of the trench too soon in the '66 title game with Green Bay, which cost them the title, and again in 1967 when Bart Starr snuck in for the game-winning touchdown in the waning moments of the Ice Bowl. Usually I place myself in a neutral role, but I got carried away during both of those games. I was rooting for Dallas because I disliked Green Bay like I used to dislike the Yankees when I rooted for the Indians and Red Sox. I just don't care for the top dog unless I'm a part of it, and in the 1960s, the top dog was Green Bay."

In 1978 Jack began a long broadcasting relationship with former Kansas City Chiefs coach Hank Stram on CBS radio. For 18 years they broadcast the top games of the week, on Monday nights, as well as postseason and Super Bowl games. They first met when Jack was

> **"Usually when the operator wakes me, I put the phone down and doze a bit longer, but when she told me how cold it was outside, I was jolted into reality. By the time I got to Lambeau Field at 10:30, it had started to warm up, to 17 below. By game time it was 15 below, and I was out of business."** —Jack Buck

Christensen's eyes took in all of the action on the Golden Gopher field. ***Photo courtesy of Ray Christensen***

2000, to kick off the season against Louisiana-Monroe, it marked Christensen's 500th Gophers football broadcast, which was noted by a halftime presentation and standing ovation from the Gopher faithful. Like many great broadcasters who worked in a regional setting, Ray Christensen is not a household name on a national scale, but in his home state of Minnesota, his name is magic.

His career began in the basement studio of Minnesota's student station, KUOM, and he was hooked from the outset. He began as the station's music director. In 1951, the athletic department needed someone to broadcast the games for nothing.

"That happened to be my price, and I applied for the job. A couple of weeks went by, and on the Monday of the first game at Washington I hadn't heard anything, so I called athletic director Ike Armstrong's office. 'Oh yes,' said his secretary, 'I've been meaning to call you. You can't charge over $2.50 a meal while you're on the road with the Gophers.' That's how I learned I was the voice of the Gophers. It ended 50 years and 510 football games later." Ray liked the fact that, unlike television, radio is a "theater of the mind. You can make it whatever you want to." All throughout the roll call of Gopher greats, from Paul Giel, Rick Upchurch, and Sandy Stephens to Darrell Thompson and Tyrone Carter, Christensen was behind the mike.

doing ABC games with Paul Christman in the early years of the AFL. Their association was similar to the one Curt Gowdy had with Paul Christman, Lindsey Nelson had with Red Grange, and Pat Summerall had with John Madden. "There isn't a day that he doesn't pop into my mind, and I remember some of the things that we did together," Stram said. "He was an artist and took great pride in what he did and how he did it."

Jack Buck passed away from complications from Parkinson's disease on June 19, 2002, at age 77.

Ray Christensen

For 50 seasons, not all of them golden, Ray Christensen was the golden voice of the Minnesota Golden Gophers. When he took the air on September 2,

Revered for his distinctive voice and flawless play calling, Christensen's beginnings as a broadcaster were in his home making up imaginary baseball games and then calling games as a spectator from the bleachers at Nicollet Park, home of the Minneapolis Millers. Enlisting in the Army in April 1942, Ray landed on the beaches of Normandy on June 10, 1944, four days after the historic Allied invasion. After the war, he returned to the University of Minnesota, determined to make radio and broadcasting his career. He began in May 1946, as a full-time announcer on KUOM. In 1951 he landed the job as play-by-play announcer for Gophers football. Although he also broadcast Minneapolis Lakers basketball, Vikings football from 1966 to 1969, Twins baseball, and 1,278 Gopher basketball games over a 44-year span, it was on football Saturdays that he did his greatest and most enjoyable work. "College football has an atmosphere that is like no other. It surrounds you. It's wonderful."

His most memorable Gophers broadcast was the November 1986 game in which Minnesota played the unbeaten Wolverines in Michigan Stadium before more than 100,000 fans. Quarterback Rickey Foggie refused

Christensen was in the booth for 50 years, covering Minnesota football. *Ad and photo courtesy of Ray Christensen*

to accept the omnipotent stature of the Wolverines and kept the Gophers in the game when many thought it would be a blowout. "Foggie's last gasp, a fourth-quarter, 31-yard run to the Wolverines' 17-yard line set the stage for Chip Lohmiller's 30-yard field goal as time expires giving Minnesota a 20-17 victory, silencing the crowd of 104,000." In recollecting the game many years later, Ray remembered the still as "the most beautiful silence I have ever heard. I'll never forget the silence."

The 24-23 win at Penn State in 1999 was also a highlight. "It was more than beating the second-ranked Nittany Lions on their Homecoming, knocking them out of the national championship picture. It was a great win for Glen Mason's program, one of the turning points."

Another highlight was in his final season of 2000 when the Gophers upset Ohio State in Columbus. "In my 50 years, Columbus was the only location I had never broadcast a victory. The Gophers beat the Buckeyes decisively that day, and my record was complete."

Paul Giel with Ray Christensen. *Photo courtesy of Ray Christensen*

description. Fans lucky enough to sit within earshot of Ray at a future game can only hope the master decides to brush up on his skills right there in the stands. Just like he did at old Nicollet Park."

Not one to extol his own personality and take away from the game, Ray always considered himself a vehicle for telling people what happened in the game. "The great compliment for me is when people say to me, 'Ray Christensen, I felt like I was there.' Then I really ask no more. That is all the eulogy I want."

Ken Coleman

Ken Coleman broadcast every one of Jim Brown's 2,359 carries, 262 receptions, and 126 touchdowns in nine seasons with the Cleveland Browns.

Coleman, the voice of the Browns on radio and television from 1952 to 1965, described every one of Brown's 12,312 yards rushing. He broadcast four title games with Otto Graham at the helm, and two more in 1964 and 1965 when the Browns upset the Baltimore Colts 27-0 and lost at Green Bay in 1965.

Coleman broke into radio after World War II, attending Curry College and getting his first job on station WSYB in Rutland, Vermont. His big break came when Paul Brown selected him to be the television voice of the Cleveland Browns in 1952, an association that lasted 14 years under Brown and later under Blanton Collier. "Paul Brown insisted I live like the

In 50 seasons, Ray worked with a lengthy list of color men, including players Paul Giel and Darrell Thompson and for 15 years former Northwestern standout Paul Flatley. Former coaches Murray Warmath and Cal Stoll also assisted Ray over the decades.

His voice is remembered with reverence in the Land of a Thousand Lakes. David La Vaque wrote in the *Minnesota Daily*: "The majestic whole of Christensen's career dwarfs his considerable skills—his ability to call the fast-moving game of football with the precision of a metronome; his voice rising to a crescendo with the count-off of yards to a player's touchdown; the appropriate, yet subtle adjectives included in a play's

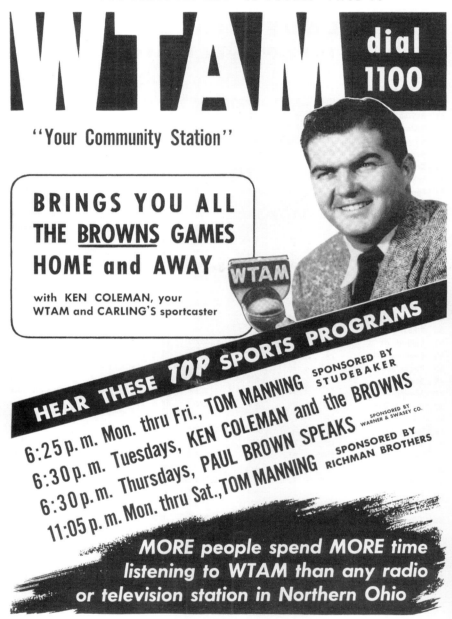

Coleman was the voice of the Browns for 14 seasons; Coleman (below) plays center with Milt Plum as Bobby Mitchell and Jim Brown look on. *Ad courtesy of WTAM; photo courtesy of the author's collection*

players at training camp, in a Hiram College dorm room," Coleman recalled about the thorough Cleveland coach. "It was Paul's idea that if I was going to broadcast Cleveland Browns football, I should learn as much about the players and the game as I could. It was a great education and one of the best breaks I ever had. I knew a little about football or I wouldn't have gotten

Ken Coleman at work covering the Cleveland Browns.
Photo courtesy of the author's collection

the job, but by the time that 1952 training camp ended, I think I could have become a coach."

Ken went on to broadcast seven NFL title games involving the Browns. During the season he hosted the weekly *Quarterback Club* on local Cleveland television, narrating the highlights of that week's game and interviewing top players. When Ken joined the Browns' TV booth, he was succeeded on radio by Gib Shanley, who announced Browns football with fervor for 20 years, many of which were assisted by Cleveland TV sports anchor Jim Graner. Shanley himself became a popular sports anchor on Cleveland television for many years.

Besides the Browns, Ken broadcast Indians baseball on television for 10 years and spent another 21 with the Red Sox, starting a year before the Impossible Dream season of 1967 and the other near misses of 1975 and 1986. Ken Coleman, revered and renowned in both Cleveland and all throughout New England, died unexpectedly on August 21, 2003, at age 78.

Howard Cosell

He was caustic, abrasive, opinionated, and full of himself. There has never been anybody quite like him, and there will never be another like him. Howard Cosell "told it like it was" like nobody before or since. *Monday Night Football* was never the same after he left it. Cosell, quite frankly, didn't want to be a part of this salute to sportscasting's "Golden Voices." He didn't want to be lumped together with play-by-play announcers who he felt were shills and salesmen. "It may be a great and romantic venture to look back upon the age of, bless them, Ted Husing, who was a very great man at what he did; Bill Stern, who I consider one of the finest dramatic performers of all time; or Graham McNamee and the others. There's nothing wrong with this. It's nostalgic, it's historic, and it's fine. But it's not related to journalism, and journalism is my main concern."

Cosell never did football play by play, yet when ABC's Roone Arledge was picking the announcing team for the league's grand new experiment, *Monday Night Football*, in 1970, Cosell was the first announcer he hired. Arledge figured prime time was different than a Sunday afternoon, and what better way to spark some controversy and add some color, than to hire Cosell to go along with Keith Jackson and Don Meredith. As it turned out, the team of "Dandy Don" and "Humble Howard," became a bigger show than the games themselves, which oftentimes were boring. Howard let Meredith, Frank Gifford, and O.J. Simpson talk about the technicalities. Cosell talked about the trappings, the stadium, the host city, the coaches, and the players. His halftime descriptions of the previous day's games, (He could go...all...the...way) were often imitated but never duplicated. On Monday nights in the fall, Cosell had the nation's stage. "Howard takes the position that what goes on on the field is an otherwise useless interruption of a brilliant monologue which he delivers in gusts of syllables like smoke rings," Jim Murray wrote in his syndicated column. "Cosell is ABC's shock theatre, the electronic cattle prod. He comes on like the guy who opens the door in the spooky old mansion in the thunderstorm and tells the standard young couple to select any coffin they want to sleep in. You're sure he'll be drinking blood by the fourth quarter. It's not whether you won or lost. It's how Howie called the game."

Born on March 25, 1918, in Winston-Salem, North Carolina, Howard Cohen (he changed it to Cosell while in college) grew up wanting to become an attorney, a goal he eventually reached. Growing up in Brooklyn, he was the sports editor of the high school paper. He went on to NYU and a law degree, admitted to the bar in 1939. Sports broadcasting was not the field he would have chosen. Oddity and circumstance played a big role.

Howard Cosell (center) "told it like it was" behind the mike. *Photo courtesy of NBC*

In the mid-1950s Howard, then 36 years old, was practicing law and was representing Little League baseball in the New York area. "In 1954 the American Broadcasting Company called me in reference to using the name 'Little League' on a network radio show they were preparing to initiate. I gave them permission on a noncommercial basis. They then asked me if I would host the show, and I said yes, more as a lark than having any desire to broadcast. But I found out I liked broadcasting very much, primarily because of its immediacy. I am, in my opinion, a born reporter. So what started out as a lark, a Saturday morning hobby, resulted in about a year's time, in a firm offer from ABC. I decided to leave my law practice and become a sports broadcaster."

Broadcasting was the right business for Cosell. He was an extrovert. In fact the only facet of law that he really enjoyed was trying a case in a courtroom. He wasn't cut out for the time-consuming process of preparing pleadings, exams before trials, and other mundane facets of the profession. He did appreciate the law background for his work in broadcasting. "Legal training will help anyone in any line of endeavor. It teaches one to think, it teaches one to analyze, it teaches one to weigh and evaluate, and it teaches one the art of expression."

Long before his 13-year run on *Monday Night Football*, Cosell was making an imprint in sports in America by his association with the then-brash boxer from Louisville, Cassius Clay. It was a time of turbulence with the Vietnam War and the Civil Rights Movement. When Clay joined the Muslim faith and changed his name, Cosell was one of the few to call him Ali. While others scorned Ali for refusing military service, Cosell was there beside him.

Cosell manned the booth for *Monday Night Football* for 13 years. Here he stands shortly before kickoff of the Dallas Cowboys-New York Giants game in 1971. ***Photo provided by AP/WWP***

Although he was a regular on *Wide World of Sports* and had a daily commentary on ABC radio, as well as a Sunday program, *Speaking of Everything*, it was *Monday Night Football* that made Cosell an American icon. Cosell helped an iffy experiment become part of American culture. The games were a perfect backdrop for his brand of blather and bluster. You either loved him or hated him, which was born out in a 1970s *TV Guide* poll that had him the most hated and most loved sportscaster, all at the same time. Cosell had few friends among the sportswriters who he chastised for being shills and in the owners' pockets. It was Red Smith who once said, "I have tried hard to like Howard Cosell, and I have failed."

After 13 years Cosell left the Monday night booth, calling pro football "a stagnant bore." *MNF* has tried ever since to come up with announcing combinations to recapture the past glory. That is impossible because there was only one Howard Cosell. Gifford lasted 28 years on the broadcast. All together there have been 20 different broadcasters on *MNF*. "I feel I have been a trailblazer, a pioneer, since my mission has concerned itself with ethics and revealing the truth within sport. I have been an electronic first, an electronic journalist, and it may be my survival in this jungle of mediocrity will be my greatest accomplishment."

It was front-page news when Howard Cosell died of cancer on April 23, 1995, at age 76.

Jack Drees

One of the tallest sportscasters ever, Jack Drees was also one of its most multifaceted, taking his abilities into a realm few announcers have ventured,

horseracing. Drees became one of the truly great race callers in the business in the 1950s and 1960s. Standing six foot, six inches at the age of 16, Drees stood out like a gawky freak in his native Chicago. In 1934 not many kids grew to that height. Jack used it to his advantage, however, playing basketball at the University of Iowa.

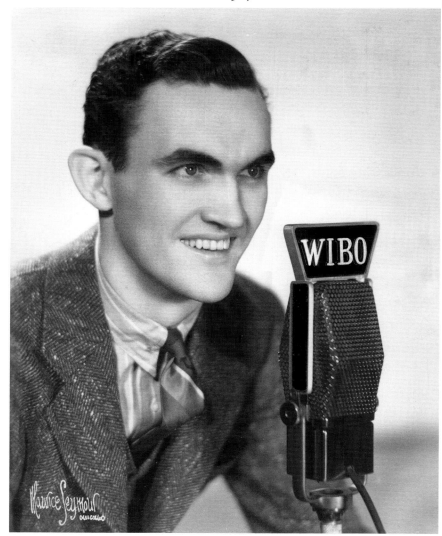

Jack Drees in 1942. *Photo courtesy of the author's collection*

There were no scholarships in the Depression, but Iowa helped Drees find a job to help him through. "I worked three hours a day washing dishes in an Iowa City restaurant to pay for my meals," Jack remembered. "I made $10 a month for sweeping two gymnasiums, and since my room rent was eight dollars a month, I had two dollars left over every month to spend." Studying for classes became difficult because of work requirements, which meant Jack had to lessen his class load in order to pass.

One of Jack's teammates on the Iowa basketball team was legendary football hero Nile Kinnick. "He only played one year," Jack said, "because it cut too deeply into his study time and the academic goals he set." Broadcasting Drees's games in those years was young Ronald "Dutch" Reagan of WHO, Des Moines. "The only contact I had with the future president was on a player-announcer relationship. During a game his flaming red hair wasn't hard to spot as he sat propped in front of the microphone, completely immersed in the ballgame."

Drees's radio career began on the student station at Iowa, automatically becoming the sports announcer because "I had been the first athlete that had ever poked his nose through the door."

Upon graduation, Drees got a big break, joining WJJD in Chicago at $35 a week, broadcasting baseball with veteran announcer John Harrington on Cubs and White Sox home games.

In the fall of 1938, Drees broadcast Big Ten football along with the pro games of the NFL Chicago Cardinals. In the fall of 1939 he switched over to the Bears games when the Bears were the Monsters of the Midway, the most dominant team in the league. He remained with the Bears until war broke out late in 1941.

The war dealt Drees a severe blow to his sportscasting career. "I hadn't established myself in Chicago to the point of being a household name, far from it, but yet I felt I was right at the threshold of becoming an established local personality when the Japanese bombed Pearl Harbor." Jack enlisted in the navy and out of 35 months served, 33 were at sea serving as a gunnery officer on a merchant ship, in charge of a 28-man gun crew. Throughout that entire 33-month period, Jack and his crew never fired a shot in anger. "While traveling in convoys, we were under submarine attack on a few occasions, but our ship escaped unscathed, although several other ships were destroyed."

Drees rejoined WIND, the sister station of WJJD, at war's end, but by that time the station had given up its sports schedule. He soon joined Ben Lindheimer, who owned Arlington Park as well as the Los Angeles Dons of the old All-America Football Conference. His duties entailed calling horse races, public relations work, and working in the Dons' front office during the football season. He didn't do Dons games because as business manager of the team, he felt it a conflict of interest if he broadcast the games. After the AAFC folded, he returned to the racetracks of Chicago and began working in the new medium of television in 1952 as one of the broadcasters on the *Pabst Wednesday Night Fights*.

In the early 1950s Jack broadcast college football on radio, and in 1954, when ABC was awarded the NCAA television rights, he and Tom Harmon broadcast the games. In 1960 he was tabbed by CBS to broadcast the games of football's St. Louis Cardinals, who had just moved from Chicago. "This came about because of the death of Joe Boland, who along with Paul Christman had formed, in my opinion, the greatest football announcing duo that ever was. Joe's death was a tragic, shocking occurrence. It created a sudden void, and I was picked to fill it."

For sheer excitement and drama, the 33-33 tie between the title-bound Browns and the Cardinals in 1964 was the ultimate thriller for Drees. "It was a rare game in which both teams played outstanding football. There weren't any lucky breaks or mental lapses that produced touchdowns. I can still see Frank Ryan of Cleveland hitting Gary Collins with the familiar post pattern at the goal line to send the Browns ahead 33-30 with just seconds left. Somehow the Cardinals got in field-goal range for Jim Bakken to tie it at the end."

The most memorable game Jack ever witnessed was the 1940 NFL title game in which the Bears devoured the Redskins 73-0. "I broadcast the game in Washington, and it was just totally unreal. It had only been two weeks earlier that Washington had beaten the Bears 7-3. In the 73-0 holocaust I believe I could have climbed out of the broadcast booth, walked into the Bear backfield, and thrown a pass somewhere that would have been caught for a touchdown. Everything the Bears touched turned to points that day."

Jack Drees continued to broadcast pro football and major league baseball throughout the 1970s. Drees died on July 27, 1988, at age 71.

Dick Enberg, who is at home covering any sport, has announced eight Super Bowls, nine Rose Bowls, and six Orange Bowls. *Photo provided by Al Messerschmidt/WireImage.com*

Dick Enberg

Dick Enberg is comfortable doing any sport, from pro football, to major league baseball, to Wimbledon tennis, to the Masters golf tournament. For 25 years Enberg announced pro football on NBC, and when NBC lost the games to Fox, he joined CBS where he serves, teamed with Dan Dierdorf, as their prime play-by-play announcer. He was described as NBC's "decathlete," for the wide range of events he's reported. A veteran of eight Super Bowls, nine Rose Bowls, and six Orange Bowls, Enberg remains one of the top guys in the business in an era watered down by what seems like hundreds of homogenized broadcasters, all looking and sounding the same.

Teamed with Merlin Olsen, John Brodie, or Bob Trumpy, Enberg broadcast 20 AFC championship games. As the winner of 13 Emmy Awards, Enberg celebrates his 50th year as a sportscaster in 2004.

Enberg succeeded Bob Kelley as the Rams' radio voice. Younger and more excitable, he'd let out an "Oh, my!" on a big play, and it became his trademark. "It's a Midwestern term. My mother used to say it all the time. I wanted a catchphrase similar to Red Barber's 'Oh doctor,' and Mel Allen's 'How about that.'"

The Armada, Michigan, native began broadcasting while a student at his alma mater, Central Michigan University. His first broadcast was announcing a semi-pro baseball game. In the second inning a player broke his ankle trying to break up a double play, and because the team only had nine men in uniform, the game was called. "I tried to say goodbye gracefully, unhooked the wires, packed the equipment, and wondered if Red Barber really started this way." He earned a master's and a doctoral degree in health sciences from Indiana University.

Dick had entered college with hopes of becoming a teacher and taught and coached for four years at Cal State Northridge before going into broadcasting. He began his full-time sportscasting career in 1965 in Los Angeles, becoming the voice of the Los Angeles Rams, UCLA basketball, and later Angels baseball. His first national exposure was as the host of *Sports Challenge*, a quiz show that pitted legendary athletes, coaches, and managers against each other in trivia contests.

His number-one sports thrill and event? John Elway's 98-yard drive to force overtime in the AFC championship game in January 1987 that saw the Broncos beat the Browns in overtime.

Jack Fleming

"Hold onto your hats, here come the Steelers out of the huddle. It's down to one big play…fourth down and 10 yards to go. Bradshaw's running out of the pocket, looking for somebody to throw to. …He fires it downfield, and there's a collision! And it's caught out of the air! The ball is pulled in by Franco Harris! Harris is going for a touchdown for Pittsburgh!"

—Jack Fleming's call of the Immaculate Reception, Steelers-Raiders playoff game, 1972

Jack Fleming was a faithful Steelers and Mountaineers football fan. *Photo courtesy of the* **University of West Virginia**

Steeler announcer Jack Fleming's call of the dramatic Immaculate Reception was described by NFL Films as the most replayed moment in pro football history, although Johnny Unitas's handoff to Alan Ameche to win the sudden-death title game in 1958 might give it a run for its money. Fleming had two allegiances in his announcing career, the Pittsburgh Steelers and the West Virginia Mountaineers. Fleming did Mountaineer football and basketball for 42 years, beginning in 1947. His tenure with the Steelers was much less, "only" 28 years, as he replaced the legendary Joe Tucker and carried on until 1993 when Bill Hillgrove took over.

Fleming had a deep-seated loyalty to West Virginia, and the fans reciprocated. "Whenever you'd go to the stadium for a game, you would see a lot of people with portable radios, all listening to Jack," longtime friend

Jack Fleming covered Mountaineers football for 28 years. *Photo courtesy of the University of West Virginia*

Jack Lynch said. "You could almost do away with the public address announcer, because you could hear Jack from the radios."

Unlike Joe Tucker, who broadcast one losing season after another with the Steelers, Fleming announced four Super Bowls, all Pittsburgh triumphs. The Morgantown native was also one of the best basketball play-by-play men in the business, even announcing many of Jerry West's high school tournament games. "I came here in 1980, and he was literally 'Mr. Mountaineer,'" longtime football coach Don Nehlen said. "Everybody in the state of West Virginia identified with Jack Fleming."

A seven-time winner of the state of West Virginia Sportscaster of the Year Award, Fleming also received, in 1999, the Chris Schenkel Award, which honors great careers in college football broadcasting and is sponsored by the National Football Foundation and College Football Hall of Fame.

After 47 years, Jack Fleming retired in 1996. He passed away on January 3, 2001. He was 77.

Marty Glickman

Another ex-athlete of renown who became an accomplished sportscaster was the "Boy From Syracuse," Marty Glickman. Marty's identifiable Brooklyn accent gave a special feel, whether it was announcing a Knicks game from the Garden, a Giants game from Yankee Stadium, or a Jets game from Shea Stadium.

An enthusiastic fan, Marty carved quite a swath from the playgrounds of Brooklyn, to the track and field heights at Syracuse University, to the 1936 Olympics in Berlin where he competed as a sprinter against the Third Reich with teammates like Jesse Owens and

Track 22; Tracks 24-26

Ralph Metcalfe. He and a teammate, Sam Stoller, however, were yanked from the Olympics because as Jews they were seen as an affront to Adolf Hitler.

Coaches Lawson Robertson and Dean Cromwell, ignoring the protests of Marty and Jesse, didn't tell them why Marty and Sam were being benched. They had to watch the four-by-100-meter relay, which the United States won by 15 yards.

Born in Brooklyn in 1917 Marty grew up playing such big-city games as punch ball, stickball, and ringaleeveo. While a student at James Madison High, he played all sports, excelling in track and football. In football he was voted to the All-City and All-State teams as a halfback. Running sprints on the track team

Marty Glickman covered the New York Giants for WNEW and was so synonymous with Giants football that WNEW ran this ad. *Photo and ad courtesy of WNEW*

Who's the Giant on the right?

He's WNEW's Marty Glickman
—a broadcaster who lives
with his team. Hear Marty,
Al DeRogatis, and Chip Cipolla
call every play of every game
—sometimes before it happens.

WNEW/1130
102.7 FM / METROMEDIA RADIO
N.Y. GIANTS FOOTBALL STATION

led to the city, state, and national schoolboy titles in 1934. He ran the 60-yard dash at Madison Square Garden, the 50-yard sprint at the Boston Garden, and of course, ran alongside Jesse Owens in the Olympics. "My top time in the 100-yard dash was 9.5 seconds," Marty recounted proudly. "That was just a tenth of a second behind Jesse."

He enrolled at Syracuse as a pre-med student, switched to political science, and came out a broadcaster, the first in a long line of Syracuse announcing alumni that includes his protégé and successor on the Knicks, Marv Albert, as well as Bob Costas, Dick Stockton, Andy Musser, and Hank Greenwald. "Before my junior year at Syracuse, the closest I had ever ventured to a microphone was as a guest on Stan Lomax's show on WOR," Marty said. "I had listened to Ted Husing, Graham McNamee, and Bill Stern but never dreamed of following in their path."

During his junior year in 1937, Marty had a big day as the Orangemen upset heavily favored Cornell 14-6. Cornell's featured player was All-America end Brud Holland, who later became president of Howard University. "I scored both touchdowns, including one on a punt return and intercepted two passes," Marty said. "With my new-found fame, a local haberdasher asked me to do a radio show on WSYR, which he would sponsor. I told him he had the wrong guy because I was nervous, stuttered, stammered, and had never been on the air before. When he offered me $15 a show I jumped at it. That first show was all I needed. The bug hit, and I was converted to radio." His first show was on at 9:15 p.m., and for five hours Marty worked on the script and polishing his delivery, writing, revising, and reworking. "I crashed before takeoff as my

first words were, 'Good afternoon, everyone.' The only sad thing was it was pitch dark outside."

Upon graduation in 1939, Marty returned to New York City and a sports job on the old WHN. His bosses were former Syracuse athlete Dick Fishell and Bert Lee, who had been a star athlete at Cornell. His first play-by-play opportunity came in the 1939 Melrose track meet at Madison Square Garden. Marty had competed in the meet as a high school senior, so he was familiar with the athletes and events. He worked off a cramped, hanging gondola on the edge of the first mezzanine, joined by color man Joe O'Brien, long a fixture on the New York sports scene. "I was terribly uncomfortable and notably nervous but survived to do the rest of the meets at the Garden for the 1939-1940 season."

When the baseball ban was listed on broadcasting major league baseball in the New York region, Marty got a job on WMGM writing a condensed game of the day, a capsule 15-minute recreation complete with crowd noise and the crack of the bat. "Bert Lee was the broadcaster," Marty said, "but he often asked me to fill in since this was a seven days a week show that went 12 years. I was getting experience and exposure."

WHN, which later became WMGM, was one of the top sports stations in the country, doing Dodger baseball, Giants and Army football, pro and college basketball, hockey, track meets, harness races, and prize fights. Until television encroached, WMGM was a sports fan's dream. Some of the best known announcers in the business broke in at WMGM: Chris Schenkel came in from Providence to begin his illustrious career, and Bud Palmer retired from the Knicks and became Marty's color man on Knicks broadcasts. Established announcers such as Red Barber,

Connie Desmond, Sam Taub, and Curt Gowdy worked for the station, and Johnny Most came up from North Carolina to join Marty and others doing New York college and pro games.

Marty was gaining valuable experience until World War II interrupted his life. Instead of calling games at Madison Square Garden, he was seeing marine combat in the Marshall Islands. "I was a night fighter controller, using a microphone to help intercept raiding enemy planes. My radio background helped me get commissioned, and they felt the fact I had been an ad-lib, play-by-play announcer, would prove helpful. It did benefit me, as I kept somewhat in the groove and didn't have to start over after three years away from the radio booth."

Basketball was Marty's bailiwick after the war, and he worked hard to be the best in the sport, soon becoming the voice of basketball in the East.

In 1948 Marty was given the opportunity to replace Connie Desmond on the football broadcasts of the New York Giants. This came about over a conflict between beer sponsors. Schaeffer beer footed the bill for the Dodger baseball broadcasts while Pabst had bought the rights to the Giant football games. Desmond was a mainstay with Red Barber on the Dodgers, so Glickman became the voice of the Giants and continued, except for a four-year span, for 23 years. He followed by doing the Jets for another 11 years, his second tour from 1988 through the 1992 season, after which he said goodbye at age 74.

As one of the first sportscasting specialists, Marty worked just about every sport imaginable on countless outlets, network, and otherwise. "Track meets, wrestling, harness racing, and even rodeos. My motto was always, 'Say it as I see it.' There was the inbred rooting interest for the Knicks or Giants, but I tried to remain objective in describing the magnificent ball carrying of Leroy Kelly and Jim Taylor and the passing brilliance of Johnny Unitas. I say what I see and leave it at that."

Of all the sports Marty broadcast, football was his favorite. "On every play there is potentially a game-winning development. It combines speed, artistry, and violence into one package."

After Marty's death in 2001, former Giant coach Allie Sherman, told a story that Marty lined up and outran all of the other Giant running backs in a foot race. He was 46 years old at the time.

Marty Glickman passed away from complications from heart bypass surgery on January 3, 2001. He was 83 years old.

Curt Gowdy

When you read the roll call of all-time great sports broadcasters, you won't wait long to hear the name Curt Gowdy. For almost 20 years, from the early 1960s to the 1980s, Curt ranked at the top of the heap. He was a mainstay on ABC, and then went to NBC, broadcasting every major event in sports, from major league baseball, pro and college football, NCAA basketball, the Olympics, and the long-running *American Sportsman*, which was his pride and joy. Those fishing forays with Ted Williams and duck hunting trips with Bing Crosby and Phil Harris were classics.

The "Cowboy at the Mike" was born in Green River, Wyoming, and brought up in Cheyenne, where he was an All-State basketball player. At the University of Wyoming, along with teammate Kenny Sailors, he

Curt Gowdy and partner Paul Christman cover the action at Pitt Stadium. *Photo courtesy of NBC*

helped spark the Cowboys to a Rocky Mountain Conference championship and an NIT bid. He was a one-handed set shot artist for Coach Ev Shelton. He won eight letters in all at Wyoming—three in basketball, three in baseball, and two in tennis.

His interest in sports led him to sportswriting for the *Wyoming Eagle* and then into broadcasting. His first play-by-play assignment was to broadcast a six-man football game in Cheyenne between St. Mary's High School and Pine Bluff High on a bitterly cold November afternoon. The game took place on a barren, vacant lot about four blocks from his home. The portable amplifier was placed on a rickety soapbox at midfield, and Curt and his engineer-commercial man, Dick Lane, sat on folding chairs describing a field without yard markers and uniforms without numbers. "The thermometer was down around zero," Curt remembered, still shivering at the memory. "Between the cold and the nervousness, my teeth were chattering. When the teams came out, I couldn't tell one from the other. There were no stands and only about 15 spectators, 14 relatives of the players and me. My voice cracked at first, but soon I was talking in conversational tones, just as if I was sitting in my room at the house, talking into my imaginary mike. I've done World Series, Olympic games, and football bowl games—events that drew 100,000 people in the stands

Gowdy in 1950. *Photo courtesy of Curt Gowdy*

and millions of listeners and viewers on television. I never see a big crowd without thinking of the 15 hardy souls who went out on a cold November day in 1943 to watch St. Mary's of Cheyenne play Pine Bluff for the six-man championship of eastern Wyoming."

Severe back pains from driving an old Model A jalopy, led to a crippling, ruptured disc while going through army calisthenics in 1942. He eventually received a medical discharge with spinal arthritis early in 1943 and entered the Mayo Clinic for an operation. The back problems have persisted through his entire adult life.

After his military service, Curt returned to Cheyenne and a job on KFBC, the local outlet, at a salary of $18 a week. His big break came when he drove to Denver to broadcast the AAU basketball championships. During one of the broadcasts, Ken Brown, the general manager of KOMA, a 50,000-watt radio station in Oklahoma City was driving through Cheyenne and heard Gowdy's description. The two soon met, but two months went by before Brown called in August 1945 to offer Curt the job of broadcasting the University of Oklahoma football games on KOMA

Curt broadcast Oklahoma football from 1945 to 1949 at a time when the Sooners were undergoing a coaching transition with Jim Tatum taking over in 1946 and Bud Wilkinson in 1947. Curt's back pains persisted, not helped by an auto accident while returning from a 1945 Sooner game at Nebraska. He had a spinal fusion operation that shelved him for six months. "They had to carry me up to the broadcasting booth during the 1946 football season," Curt said. "I was living on codeine and sleeping pills."

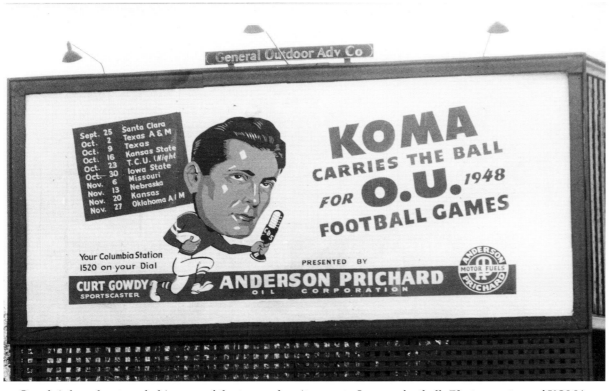

Gowdy's broadcast made him one of the team when it came to Sooners football. *Photo courtesy of KOMA*

Gowdy's first coast-to-coast broadcast occurred in 1948 when Oklahoma played Texas Christian. The game was picked up on Red Barber's *CBS Roundup*. Oklahoma won the game, and the whole country was beginning to take notice of the Sooners, who were in the midst of a 31-game win streak. Gowdy was equally popular, having the biggest following of any broadcaster ever to work in Oklahoma. "Football broadcasting is hardest of all," Gowdy told a reporter in 1948. "You've got 22 men to take care of, and you're high in the stadium, where it's hard to see them hide the ball. You've got to do lots of quick mental arithmetic. The mass substitution is hard to follow. If some guy scores a touchdown and you haven't got him in the game, the fans want to mob you."

In 1947, there were rumors that Curt was going to leave Oklahoma for a big league baseball announcing job and Wheaties sponsored a "Keep Curt Gowdy in Oklahoma City" campaign. It worked for two more years.

While broadcasting Oklahoma City Texas League games in 1948, Gowdy came into contact with Jack Slocum, son of the esteemed baseball writer Bill Slocum. Slocum was working for Knox-Reeves advertising and the Wheaties account. Jack had formerly been radio director of the New York Yankees and recommended Curt to Mel Allen after Russ Hodges departed the Yankee booth for the nearby Polo Grounds as chief announcer of the Giants. Two months went by before George Weiss called to say the list of 300 candidates had been whittled down to three. The other two, Curt believes, were Bud Foster and Larry Ray.

Curt got the nod, and in 1949 launched his major league announcing career. In 1951 he became the chief announcer of the Boston Red Sox, and in 1961 began an eight-year football broadcasting partnership with Paul Christman that developed into one of the greatest sportscaster combinations in history. "Even though we were broadcasting AFL games in the league's infancy,

Gowdy moved from KOMA and Sooners football to covering some of football's best games; Gowdy (right) and Christman (center) prepare for an Orange Bowl telecast. *Ads courtesy of KOMA; photo courtesy of the University of Miami*

Gowdy and Christman were the faces and voices of the AFL. *Photos courtesy of NBC*

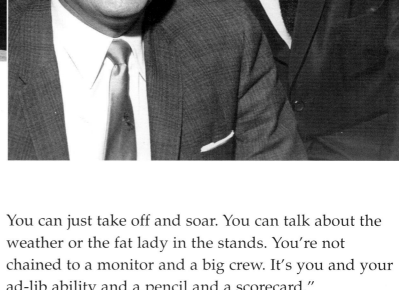

we became identifiable with the public," Curt remembered. "We struggled for six years with the AFL but still managed to develop a national reputation. When Paul left me to go to CBS, I really believe he broke up something special. We went together hand in glove. We offset each other and understood each other. Roone Arledge actually thought we were bigger than the league itself, which I disagreed with. He said many people would tune in just to listen to us, not caring about the game."

Curt left the Red Sox after the 1965 season to join NBC and broadcast network baseball and AFL football. His days on radio were over, and he regretted it. "It's the most fulfilling job in sports. You're like a wild bird.

You can just take off and soar. You can talk about the weather or the fat lady in the stands. You're not chained to a monitor and a big crew. It's you and your ad-lib ability and a pencil and a scorecard."

Curt reached his TV peak when he announced the first Super Bowl (then called the NFL-AFL Championship) in January 1967. "It was the most unique sports day in the history of American TV," Curt said. "CBS and NBC both contracted to television the game between Green Bay and Kansas City. The

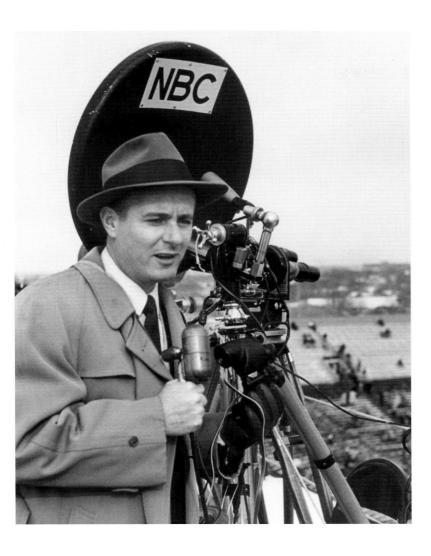

but not by much, because of the dominance and control of the major NFL markets that they enjoyed."

Millions of dollars were riding on the game, and the pressure built up all week on Curt and Paul. About five minutes before game time, Curt was left alone in the booth for a moment. "I suddenly said to myself,

Left: Gowdy broadcast the first Super Bowl for NBC. Below: Jack Kemp, Don Meredith, Johnny Unitas, and Johnny Sample stand with Curtis McLinton (hunched), Christman, Lance Alworth, and Gowdy before NBC's Super Bowl coverage. *Photos courtesy of NBC*

network battle turned out more competitive than the game itself. The networks' promotional hoopla was beyond the saturation point. There were meetings after meetings in the weeks before the game with the rival executives resembling battle staffs. The announcers, Ray Scott and Jack Whitaker for CBS, and Paul and I for NBC, got along well, but we were caught in the middle of all these strategy meetings involving everybody from General Sarnoff on down. During the game, the ratings battle became more important than the score. CBS won,

Former Packer Jerry Kramer (left) and Gowdy. *Photo provided by Vernon Biever*

"It meant the end of an era," Gowdy said. "It was the end of NFL domination over the AFL. Joe Namath changed the entire complexion of pro football. The Jets victory had the biggest single impact on pro football, television, sponsorships, and attendance since the game began. It made the American Football League."

Even though he made his mark primarily in television, Curt still prefers radio. "I love to walk into a radio both with just a microphone, an engineer, and my co-announcer because we're a combination of disc-jockeys, newsmen, sports announcers, entertainers, and commercial men. We have complete freedom."

Numerous awards and accolades have come Gowdy's way over the years. Two stand out. In 1970 he won the George Foster Peabody Award, given annually for meritorious achievements in the broadcast industry. He was the first sportscaster so honored. "Over the years Mr. Gowdy has achieved top stature with a winning blend of reportorial accuracy, a vast fund of good humor, and an infectiously honest enthusiasm for his subject. Curt Gowdy stands today at the top of his profession," the Peabody committee said. The other honor took place in March 1972, when a picturesque area outside of Cheyenne where he once hunted and fished was named Curt Gowdy State Park.

Now 85, Curt divides his time between homes in Florida and Boston. His broadcasting skills are as sharp

'Gowdy, you've broadcast football for years and have witnessed thousands of games. This is where experience is really going to help you, and you are prepared. Just report the ballgame.' And that's just what Christman and I did. I don't feel it was any better than many of the games we had done before, but knowing I had seen just about everything there was to see and knowing I had prepared thoroughly made me at ease and confident."

Curt was also behind the mike for two other unforgettable games; the 1968 Heidi Game in which the Raiders rallied for two touchdowns to beat the Jets after NBC cut out to broadcast the children's classic, *Heidi*; and the Jets' huge upset of the Colts in Super Bowl III.

today as they were when he stood alone as the top play-by-play broadcaster on the planet.

Merle Harmon

When Joe Namath led the New York Jets to a stunning upset of the Baltimore Colts in Super Bowl III, Merle Harmon was at the microphone. He was the voice of the Jets, already a seasoned veteran of more than 20 years as a baseball and football broadcaster.

*Merle Harmon was the voice of the New York Jets for nine years. **Photo courtesy of Bruno of Hollywood***

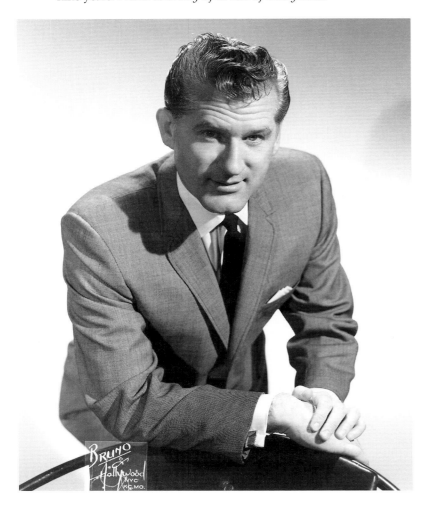

Unlike some broadcasters who fell into the profession by accident, Merle knew he wanted a career in radio right from the beginning. He graduated with a degree in radio from the University of Denver in 1949. He began his sportscasting career during his senior year at the University of Denver and 40 years later could look back on World Series and Super Bowls he covered, along with assignments for bowl games, Olympic games, and pro football. Merle was the voice of five Major League Baseball teams and for nine years was the voice of the New York Jets. *TV Guide* once wrote: "he might be the best radio football play-by-play man ever."

Born in 1926 and raised in a farm community in Salem, Illinois, Merle grew up worshipping the St. Louis Cardinal baseball team. His father went from farming to running a grocery store and was hoping Merle would run it when he returned from military service overseas in World War II. Merle thanked his father but said "no thanks" to the offer. He was 19 years old when his two-year military stint ended. After graduation from Denver, he took a job at a small station in Illinois. Before he even started, a chance drive to Topeka, Kansas, to visit a friend's friend who was the sales manager of a radio station there, changed things completely. "The friend of a friend mentioned that another station in Topeka was looking for a sports announcer," Harmon remembered.

The station was KJAY, and they needed a football announcer. At first Merle turned the offer down and reported to the station in Illinois. Before he had worked a day, KJAY called again, and this time he relented and accepted. He was there about a week when the

Harmon got his start in radio in Kansas working for several different stations; Harmon interviewed some of the biggest names in Kansas football, as well as the well-knowns of the college gridiron, including Biggie Munn (lower right). *Background photo courtesy of KCMO Radio, Susquehanna Radio Corp.; foreground photo courtesy of Merle Harmon*

Harmon (left) covers University of Kansas football in 1952. Harmon presents Paul Hornung (right) with an award in 1962. *Left photo courtesy of the University of Kansas; right photo courtesy of Merle Harmon*

manager of the minor league baseball team got into an argument with the radio broadcaster, who proceeded to quit. "All of a sudden I was the baseball announcer, even though I had never set foot in the Topeka ballpark," Merle said. Topeka at that time was a Class C team playing in the Western Association. Not only did Merle have no advance notice, the team was playing on the road, which meant he had to recreate the game by Western Union telegraph. "So that's how I started announcing baseball, with the team 200 miles

away in Muskogee, Oklahoma, and me sitting in a studio. I said originally my broadcasting career didn't happen by accident, but the baseball end of it certainly did." He went on to broadcast the Milwaukee Braves, Kansas City Athletics, Minnesota Twins, and Milwaukee Brewers.

Merle stayed in Topeka for four years before moving to WHB in Kansas City where he announced the fortunes of the Kansas City Blues, who were in their final year of operation. In 1955 he was selected to

Bruce Rice (left) and Harmon (far right) host the *All Pro Scoreboard* for ABC in 1963. **Photo courtesy of Merle Harmon**

Football began making a toehold in Merle's career in 1959 when he broadcast the Army-Air Force game at Yankee Stadium in New York. "It was the first meeting between the teams," Harmon recalled, "and it ended in a 13-13 tie." Merle contrasts baseball and football broadcasting by how the crowd reacts. "In football, when I was broadcasting a Jets game at Shea Stadium, the fans would be totally into Joe Namath. When Joe trotted off the field, the fans headed for the concession stands. If the Jets recovered a fumble and the offense was suddenly back on the field, the fans would turn around in the aisles and wait to see if the Jets

broadcast the games of the Kansas City Athletics, the major league team that had just moved from Philadelphia.

Merle continued to broadcast the A's games for the next seven years, until joining ABC in New York as a multifaceted sports announcer. In 1964 he moved to Milwaukee to broadcast the Braves games under the promise that the team wouldn't move. It did, in 1966, which meant Merle had to broadcast the lame-duck season of 1965. After sitting out the 1966 season he joined the Minnesota Twins in 1967 for one of the most stirring pennant races in baseball history.

scored or gave up the ball. They were only interested in watching that one man."

Merle feels television changed the concept of what a sports announcer is supposed to be. Television desires a more low-key broadcaster, not one who will lull the viewer to sleep, but rather give a clear, concise, report of the action. "The days of the 'screamers' have long passed," he said. "In the minor leagues I used to be a screamer, but television calmed me down and made me realize a routine play is a routine play. There is nothing else to be done with it or to try to do with it. On the other hand, a great play is a great play, and if the announcer shows excitement, the audience should react the same way. The announcer is just like the fan sitting in the stands. He is witnessing the same thing the fan is witnessing, and if he does not have the courtesy to report the facts to the listening audience, then, to me, he shouldn't be a broadcaster."

Ernie Harwell

Ernie Harwell carved a Hall of Fame career as a baseball broadcaster, parlaying his crackling voice and Southern, folksy style into a career that saw him broadcast major league baseball in seven different decades. Not many remember that Ernie also broadcast football, both pro and college.

In the mid-1950s, after coming to Baltimore as the chief announcer for the Orioles, he teamed with Chuck Thompson and Bailey Goss on Baltimore Colts radio and television broadcasts. Before that he was on the staff of Red Barber's *CBS Football Roundup*. The roundup, which began in 1948, saw Barber serve as studio host, with several announcers sent to broadcast key college games, usually from five or six games. Red would hopscotch from game to game depending on the scores and what was transpiring. The announcers would do the broadcast as if they were on the network the entire game when in reality it might be for only 20 minutes or less. "Red had two or three regulars, such as Connie Desmond and myself, and he would use announcers in different locales such as Bob Neal in Columbus, Bingo Blanchard down in Knoxville, and someone on the West Coast," Harwell

Ernie Harwell, although best known for baseball, teamed with Chuck Thompson and Baily Goss to cover Colts football. *Photo courtesy of the Baseball Hall of Fame*

remembered. "There was a set formula when Red came to you. You'd announce the score and the time, and if anything exciting happened while you were on the air, you'd keep it and do the play by play. Usually each announcer would keep it only two or three minutes and then throw it back to Red." Ernie said the demise of the

Harwell (second from left) and Goss (third from right) have a beer with Colts coach Weeb Ewbank (second from right), Colts general manager Don Kellett (far left), and National Brewery executives in honor of the Brewery sponsoring the 1955 Colts team. *Photo courtesy of the author's collection*

When he went to New York to do Brooklyn Dodger baseball in 1948, he worked with Russ Hodges on WPIX, doing Fordham, Yale, Boston College, and Boston University games. "Russ and I would go up to Boston and do a Friday night game at Fenway Park and then come down to New Haven and do the Yale game on Saturday," said Ernie. Ernie also did Yale games on the Yankee Network for several years, extending into the years he worked in Baltimore and worked Pitt football in 1952. Ernie did his share of pro football while working in New York, including the Giants, Dodgers, and Colts. "I was on hand for Brooklyn's last season of pro football in 1948," Ernie said. "I was one of their pallbearers."

CBS Roundup was caused by the cost of installing the lines into each stadium. Sponsored by Westinghouse, the *CBS Roundup* ended in the early 1950s.

Ernie began broadcasting football in 1940 as the color voice of the Rambling Wreck from Georgia Tech. Ernie assisted Marcus Bartlett, who was also the program director of WSB. Later, when the Atlantic Refining Company set up a network to do the Georgia Tech games, he did the play by play.

When he came to Detroit to join the Tigers in 1960, Ernie only did one year of football. That was in 1963 when he did Michigan State games. On the professional level, he did color for Marty Glickman on New York Giants games and did Brooklyn Dodger football in the old All-America Football Conference in 1948. "The Dodgers had 14 games that year and won only two," Harwell grimaced. "The biggest crowd at home at Ebbets Field was about 14,000 for a night game against the football Yanks. The league folded and so did my job."

On Baltimore Colts broadcasts in 1955, he alternated halves on either radio or TV with Chuck Thompson. "That was the first year of Alan Ameche, and in the first game I did, at Memorial Stadium, Ameche went 78 yards for a touchdown on his first NFL run."

Keith Jackson is the Lindsey Nelson of college football from the 1970s through today. *Photo © 2004 ABC Archives*

Except for that year doing Michigan State in 1963, it was all baseball for Ernie from there on in. In comparing baseball with football, he thinks for one game football might be harder to broadcast because of all of the preparation involved. "However baseball exposes the announcer to a greater degree, making it easier for the listener to grow tired of him. Baseball fans are so much more knowledgeable and critical than those in football," Ernie said. "Football coaches have to wait to see the film before they can tell you who played well. If the coach can't tell us, then how could anyone else be critical enough to tell us?"

After 60 years, Ernie retired from baseball play by play at age 84 after the 2002 season.

Keith Jackson

What Lindsey Nelson was to college football in the 1950s and 1960s, Keith Jackson has been to the 1970s, 1980s, 1990s, and up to the present day in fact. Fifty-two years and counting. Keith Jackson remains the voice of college football. The signature "Voice of Autumn." If Keith is calling the game, it must be a big one. With his homespun way with words and spinning a phrase, Keith Jackson has become a beloved figure on the American sports scene, and that's not easy in this era of wall-to-wall coverage where one announcer blends with the other. Keith Jackson has been accorded every accolade his profession bestows, including the National Football Foundation's Gold Medal, its highest honor. Previous winners include the likes of President John Kennedy, Jackie Robinson, and John Wayne.

No one came from more obscure surroundings to hit the big time than Keith Jackson. Born eight miles from Carrollton, Georgia, Keith attended school in a one-classroom building in Tallapoosa. He picked cotton after school and studied at night by kerosene lamp. "When I was 10 years old, my grandmother, on whose farm I grew up, told my mother one day, 'You need to talk to your son. I hear him out there in the cornfield....talking to himself.' Actually I was describing Walter Mitty's flight over the goal line in the Rose Bowl," Keith remembered.

Keith graduated from Roopville High School in 1946. Then came a four-year stint in the U.S. Marines. He was a few days short of 17 years old when he enlisted. He spent the rest of his teen years in the corps, which included time in China as an aircraft mechanic. After his discharge he enrolled at Washington State University where he began doing the Cougars play by play on station KWSC. It was in 1952 that he called his first game as the Cougars hosted Stanford, losing 14-13 on a botched extra point. Bob Mathias, who later won two Olympic decathlon gold medals, was in the Stanford backfield. He also broadcast high school football and minor league baseball for some extra money. "I did a high school game sitting in a third-floor classroom

Jackson prepares for a college football matchup.
Photo © 2004 ABC Archives

window across the street from the field," Keith said. "It was the highest perch we could find."

After graduation Keith headed to Lewiston, Idaho, to help launch a new radio station. He had another offer from established WSB in Atlanta, but Lewiston paid more money. Money, with a new wife and three children on the horizon, was something Keith was in need of. "The wheel started turning when a college chum, Dick Gardner, called to tell me there was a job for a sports guy at KOMO-TV in Seattle. I went over, got the job, borrowed a hundred bucks, and moved my bride and our belongings across the state of Washington."

After working at ABC's affiliate KOMO in Seattle for a decade; adding news to the sports chores; working 14-hour days; and doing University of Seattle basketball, Washington and Washington State football, and Pacific Coast League baseball, he joined the ABC network in 1964. "The 10 years in Seattle," Keith said, "furnished the opportunity for the foundation for the rest of my career."

Except for some work on the old *Today* show on NBC, Keith's entire network career has been with ABC, on both radio and television. His first college telecast on ABC pitted Duke at Clemson in the Atlantic Coast Conference. His color man was Jackie Jensen, a great baseball player primarily with the Red Sox but also an All-America fullback for Pappy Waldorf at California. His analysts over the years have included Bob Griese (12 years), Frank Broyles (nine years), Ara Parseghian, Bud Wilkinson, and currently, Dan Fouts. "Staying west of the big mountains has been a help," Keith said. "My body was starting to look like a well-used airplane seat."

In 1970 he was the original play-by-play voice of *Monday Night Football*, but after a year of trying to referee the antics of Howard Cosell and Don Meredith, he returned to the college game, which was his first love. His philosophy is a simple one, "Amplify, Clarify and Punctuate and let the viewer draw his or her own conclusions." Keith found time to spring himself free from football to broadcast 10 Winter and Summer Olympics. His work on *Wide World of Sports* has taken him to 31 different countries.

As the new year dawned in 1999, Keith, to paraphrase one of his favorite expressions, said, "Whoa Nellie!" retiring after broadcasting the Fiesta Bowl national championship game that saw Tennessee beat Florida State. "Nearly three decades since redefining the sound of televised college football with an evocative idiom and a storyteller's bio, he insists it is time to see whether the young bucks in his shadow are as talented as they think," Richard Sandomir wrote in *The New York Times*. How could the sameness of the "young bucks" supplant the virtuosity of the master? Fortunately the retirement was short lived as Keith decided to combine broadcasting and life in one time zone. He's

concentrated on the Pac-10 and the big bowls, especially the Rose Bowl. "I know I still enjoy doing what I do," Keith said. "I love doing college football games." Working with Bob Griese for upward of 12 years also influenced his decision to continue in the booth. "Bob does the Xs and Os and I do the shoveling," quipped Keith, who now teams with Dan Fouts.

About his down-home lingo, Keith told Sandomir, "I talk to the guy who busted his butt all week to buy a color TV, and the woman who's raising her kids, the people I owe a debt to. I'm talking to people in hotel rooms, lonesome people."

Lindsey Nelson

Of all the broadcasters who have announced football over the years, be it college or professional, none packed the verve, the voice, and the excitement of the game more than Lindsey Nelson. In the 1950s and through the 1960s, he was Mr. College Football. Teamed with his boyhood idol, the legendary Red Grange, Lindsey made Saturday afternoons in the fall something special. In those years before *SportsCenter* and before wall-to-wall coverage of games beginning Tuesday night and stretching through the week with several games on Saturday, Lindsey was the voice of the game.

Lindsey's first dose of college football was in the 1920s when he listened to college games on the West Coast when it was pitch black in his native Tennessee. Born and raised in Columbia, Tennessee, Lindsey grew up listening to Jack Harris, who broadcast Vanderbilt games on station WSM. It was Harris who helped steer Lindsey into broadcasting instead of sportswriting. He had become the sports editor of the *Columbia Daily*

Herald before he even entered college, working for free and gaining experience. When he entered the University of Tennessee, he began newspaper work in Knoxville, beginning as a morgue clerk and working up to basketball game stories.

Tennessee was enjoying great gridiron success in the late 1930s under General Bob Neyland. From 1938 through 1940, the Vols went 31-2 with three conference titles and three major bowl appearances. Lindsey began tutoring players in the football program and became so adept that he was awarded a scholarship for his tutoring expertise. Plus he immersed himself into the Tennessee football program, which was at its zenith. "In 1939 we shut out all 10 of our regular-season foes, compiling an undefeated, untied, and unscored-upon season, the last time a major college accomplished that feat," Lindsey remembered with pride.

The national radio networks began broadcasting Tennessee football in 1938, and Lindsey was tabbed to be a spotter. This was the spark that ignited his desire to become a sportscaster. He spotted for Bill Stern on several occasions, including the 1940 Rose Bowl in Pasadena. He had no place to stay in Pasadena so Knoxville sports editor Tom Anderson and Chattanooga sports editor Wirt Gammon let him stay in their room at the Huntington Hotel. When it came to meals, he would just sign their name on the card. A quarter-century later when he worked his first Rose Bowl game as a broadcaster, he checked into the Huntington and phoned Anderson in Knoxville. "I want you to know that I'm back at the Huntington," Lindsey exclaimed. "This time under my own name."

The following summer Bill Stern invited Lindsey to come to Chicago to spot the College All-Star Game. "I

Nelson led the cheers for college football during his extensive career covering the NCAA gridiron. *Photo courtesy of CBS*

was in ROTC camp in Alabama but made plans to journey to Chicago, buying a Greyhound bus ticket. Unbeknownst to me, the broadcast was canceled while I was enroute because the Vice President of the United States, Henry Wallace, was scheduled to address the nation. So I arrived in Chicago without any money. I went out to the All-Star camp to see some of the college greats, such as Nile Kinnick of Iowa, Ken Kavanaugh of LSU, Bulldog Turner of Hardin Simmons, and

Tennessee greats Bob Suffridge and George Cafego. I spent a few hours watching practice and then was faced with the problem of trying to find a place to sleep that night. I had 50 cents in my pocket, which meant I could find a room or save the half-dollar until the next morning and eat breakfast. After much deliberation I ended up buying a copy of the *Chicago Tribune* because it was the thickest paper in town, and I could spread it out on the grass down in Grant Park. I spent the night in the park, had breakfast with the 50 cents, and hitchhiked back to Tennessee. Years later I went to Chicago to attend the All-Star Game, and

Nelson (right) watches as Norm Van Brocklin (left), the quarterback for the Philadelphia Eagles, is presented by Murray Olderman with an award. ***Photo courtesy of the author's collection***

because I arrived late, the only room the Hilton could supply was about half the size of the regular rooms. Good friend and LSU athletic director Jim Corbett came over to pick me up and said, 'Gee, you didn't get much of a room did you?' 'No,' I answered, 'but it's better than Grant Park over there, and I've slept in that, too.'"

It never entered Lindsey's mind at that time that he would one day follow in the footsteps of Bill Stern on NBC football broadcasts. Lindsey patterned his announcing style after Stern—delivery, voice, inflection, intonation, and excitement. There was a time when you couldn't tell them apart. "I imitated him that closely," Lindsey said. "On New Year's Day, 1951, Bill announced the Cotton Bowl and I spotted for him as a

throwback to the prewar days. The game was on NBC, and at halftime Bill interviewed me because he said he had been told there was a fellow around broadcasting football who sounded almost exactly like him. His comment when I finished was, 'He does sound like Bill Stern, heaven forbid!'"

In Lindsey's senior year at Tennessee, he got his first real taste of sports announcing, doing the color on Volunteer games on station WNOX in Knoxville. Lowell Blanchard did the play by play. Instead of graduating and getting a big job in radio, Lindsey instead graduated in June 1941 and immediately joined an infantry platoon as a second lieutenant. His army experience was satisfying, because life was all uphill after that. "No matter whatever happens in life, it will be better," Lindsey said. "Life could never get lower than that, no matter what happened." Lindsey was in the Ninth Infantry Division, serving in North Africa, Sicily, England, France, Belgium, and Germany. "I still believe that the experience one derives from serving in a combat unit may overshadow anything else that happens in an individual's lifetime. The emotional effects will probably be greater than anything that could possibly happen anywhere."

Broadcasting opportunities weren't in abundance when he was discharged from the army. Lindsey worked at a Knoxville newspaper until he was hired to do a nightly sports show in Knoxville. In 1948 he became the voice of Tennessee football and helped form the Vol Network, which he anchored for two years before departing for Dallas and a job on Gordon McLendon's Liberty Network. Liberty, which specialized in recreating Major League Baseball games, was committed to broadcasting all of the Army games in 1950 with Ted Husing at the mike. With a week off before the traditional game with Navy, Lindsey sold McLendon on airing the Tennessee-Kentucky game, with Lindsey getting his first national exposure. Soon after, Lindsey joined Liberty full time as both a baseball and football announcer. On weekends they did six football games, beginning with the Miami Hurricanes on Friday night. They did an eastern game Saturday afternoon, a West Coast game after that, and the LSU game on Saturday night. On Sundays they did the New York Yanks and Los Angeles Rams. "We would tape the games and cross them in El Paso," Lindsey said. "So if you

Red Smith (left seated) and Nelson (right seated) are honored as the top sportswriter and sportscaster for the fourth straight year in 1962. *Photo courtesy of the author's collection*

were in the western portion of the country you heard the Rams followed by the Yanks, and if you were in the east you heard the Yanks followed by the Rams." Lindsey became Liberty's director of football, which meant he would call athletic directors, buy the rights to games if they were within the budget, and then hop on a plane and announce the game. "Unlike baseball, we did very few football recreations," Lindsey remembered. "Most of it was live." Covering football's Yanks gave Lindsey his first exposure in New York, and when he resigned from his Liberty job about three weeks before the network filed for bankruptcy, he was already talking to new NBC Sports Director Tom Gallery about being his assistant on both the radio and television networks.

Beside NBC, he also was offered a job in Cleveland to do the Browns games and was considering offers from Knoxville, Birmingham, and New Orleans, so there were plenty of fires in Lindsey's fireplace in that summer of 1952. Gallery finally made the offer official, and Lindsey joined NBC as assistant sports director, making less as he found out later than he would have made doing the Browns in Cleveland. There were a few other drawbacks: One, he was now the boss of his idol Bill Stern, which bothered Lindsey a great deal. Stern had been the only sports director that NBC ever had, and now he was relegated to just announcing duties, and two, Lindsey

was now an executive and not an on-air talent. In fact, the network's 1952 college football TV announcing team was Mel Allen, Bill Henry, and Russ Hodges. Lindsey did announce the 1952 Army-Navy game on radio and on New Year's Day in 1953 did his first Cotton Bowl game on television, the beginning of a streak that lasted more than 20 years.

In 1953 General Motors again bought the football package, and their executives asked Gallery if Lindsey could do the color. Gallery declined saying Lindsey would be too busy producing. "I was sitting there

Lindsey Nelson (center) works for the University of Tennessee's Vol Network in 1950. **Photo courtesy of the University of Tennessee**

pleading inside for Tom to say yes because I wanted to announce the games badly," Lindsey said. On the way back to New York on the train he told Gallery he would like to broadcast the games. Announcers weren't highly regarded by network executives, and Gallery was stunned by Lindsey's request. Gallery granted the request, and in the fall of 1953 he and Mel Allen were picked to do the college schedule. During that 1953 season he worked the Georgia–Florida game in Jacksonville with the old Georgia Bulldog, Bill Munday. "Bill did the color except for the second quarter when NBC agreed to let me bring him to the mike for some play by play," Lindsey remembered. "The response from the public was overwhelming. We received hundreds of wires from people all over the country saluting this great pioneer."

At the end of the 1953 season Lindsey again worked the Cotton Bowl, with Red Grange handling the color. It was his first opportunity to work with the legendary Illinois Galloping Ghost. Subsequently they worked five seasons together as a team on the college Game of the Week. In 1954, however, NBC lost the college rights to ABC, and Lindsey spent the season teamed with one of the Notre Dame Four Horsemen, Jim Crowley, broadcasting Canadian football. "I learned an awful lot from Red Grange in the five years we worked college football together, 1955 through 1959. Not only about football, but about people," Lindsey said. "Here was a man who as a college boy had been an internationally famous figure. He was perhaps the most glorified individual who ever played the game. He helped put the pro game on the map, and with all the fame, it never affected him one bit. Red was one of the finest individuals I have ever met. To

see him take the time and have the patience to meet with everyone who approached him, was incredible. He never sloughed anyone off."

Among his great memories of working with Red was the 1957 Notre Dame 7-0 upset of Oklahoma, breaking the Sooners' 47-game winning streak and the 1954 Cotton Bowl between Rice and Alabama in which Alabama's Tommy Lewis came off the bench to tackle Dickie Moegle as he was running for a touchdown. "That was my first game with Red, and in our preparation we discussed what the ruling would be if a player came off the bench and tackled a ball carrier. We discovered that this was a rare case in which a referee could award a touchdown. When it happened the very next day, a very confident Red Grange turned to me and opened the palm of his hand as if to say, 'Be my guest.' Everybody in the press box was scratching their heads and looking for a rulebook. In the NBC booth, just as I said the ref is empowered to award a touchdown if he thinks the runner would have scored, the ref shot up his arms to indicate a touchdown. By fate, we had discussed that very situation, the night before."

In 1960 ABC once again outbid NBC for the rights to college football and once again Lindsey was on the sidelines. Gallery scrambled and lined up the rights to the NFL's Pittsburgh Steelers and Baltimore Colts, which gave him his first professional football experience. Lindsey was hopscotching all over the country during this period. He would do the NFL championship in 1961 and the following day the Sugar Bowl in New Orleans. He did the Senior Bowl in Mobile followed by the U.S. Bowl in Washington. It became an endurance test. "I did seven bowl games that year," he said, shaking his head. "It got to the point where I would have to get an index card and write on it the name of the game and the city I was in and place it directly in front of me in the booth." He would soon "settle down," becoming the voice of the New York Mets in 1962, leaving NBC after a 10-year run. He packed up his spotting boards and put all of his football gear in the attic.

By the time July rolled around, however, Lindsey was getting the football "itch," and when Bill McPhail called from CBS asking him to do college football, he said yes without a hesitation. "They teamed me with Terry Brennan, and we worked together for four seasons," Lindsey said. "One of my big thrills occurred in November 1962 when Roger Staubach led Navy to a convincing 35-14 win over Army with President John F. Kennedy in the stands."

"Staubach on the keeper, being bulldogged at the 14-yard line. It's a Navy first down. The Brigade of Midshipmen is standing. Staubach throwing up the middle and it's complete. TOUCHDOWN! It's a Navy touchdown. Neil Henderson scoring from 11 yards out. That's Robert Kennedy, the Attorney General of the United States up and applauding...Staubach is going to run...to the 15, the 10, the five, TOUCHDOWN! President Kennedy...up...on his feet as the Midshipmen sing the Navy Blue and Gold."

It was 1962 and Lindsey had never broadcast a Rose Bowl. He hadn't even seen one since 1940 and said to his wife one day as they sat in the empty stands on a visit to Pasadena, "It's really the only

Nelson in the press box. ***Photo provided by Vernon Biever***

football event I wanted to work but didn't." He even decided to ask NBC—even though he was working for CBS. Perry Smith, the number-two man at NBC sports asked Lindsey to do the Rose Bowl on television. When CBS granted permission, knowing his desire to do the Rose Bowl would be the crown jewel of his career, Lindsey promptly accepted.

He would continue to broadcast college football, narrating the Notre Dame weekly recap along with the Chicago Bears highlight show, shocking the nation with his gaudy sports jackets and broadcasting Mets baseball through 1978.

Parkinson's disease began slowing Lindsey in the 1980s. He passed away on June 10, 1985, at age 76.

Chris Schenkel

Although a radio veteran, Chris Schenkel made his mark as a play-by-play telecaster, both with football's New York Giants and then as the top voice of college football, succeeding Lindsey Nelson and preceding Keith Jackson. Teamed with Bud Wilkinson, Chris was Mr. College Football in the years just before the cable explosion that permeated the airwaves with several college games every week. He was also a fixture on NBA basketball, pro bowling, and golf. His mellifluous, soothing baritone voice made viewers of the Masters golf tournament want to travel to Augusta post haste to see if it was all that Chris cracked it up to be.

But it wasn't play by play that launched Schenkel's career, but rather blow by blow. He got his start broadcasting the fights on the old Dumont Network, making the leap from his native Indiana. Born in 1923 in Wabash, Indiana, Chris was raised in Bippus, Indiana. He majored in pre-med at Purdue University

before departing for the army in 1943. By the time he was discharged in 1946, he was staging boxing tournaments in Korea. Upon his return to the states he got a sportscasting job in Providence, Rhode Island, concentrating on Brown University and Holy Cross, whose basketball team was led by the great Bob Cousy. He also did a smattering of horse racing.

Chris Schenkel was the voice of the Ivy League and the voice of the New York Giants. *Photo courtesy of CBS*

Harvard was one of the first colleges to televise football, and in 1947, 1948, and 1949, he helped pioneer football telecasting by announcing the Crimson games on NBC. In 1950 and 1951 he telecast Ivy League football over WCAU-TV in Philadelphia, and in 1952 cracked the Big Apple as the voice of the New York Giants.

The 1950s saw pro football explode into a golden era, and the Giants with Charley Conerly, Kyle Rote, Sam Huff, and Frank Gifford helped lead the way. Chris later would help several ex-Giants get their feet wet as color men on Giants broadcasts, among them Pat Summerall, Al Derogatis, Frank Gifford, and Kyle Rote. All four graduated to the networks.

Chris's debut on the network fight broadcasts came when Ted Husing was unable to continue because of illness. Husing became Schenkel's mentor, so much so that Chris named his first son Edward Britt, which was Ted's real name. His network start developed into 13 seasons of Giants football, 12 years as the voice of NCAA football on ABC, six years of *Monday Night Fights*, nine Summer and Winter Olympics from Squaw Valley to Calgary, all the major golf tournaments with "Lord Byron"— Byron Nelson—at his side, and 33 years with the Pro Bowlers Tour.

Chris did some memorable games throughout his career, including the Colts-Giants "sudden death" battle for the 1958

championship. The only one that comes close was the 1971 "Game of the Century" on Thanksgiving Day that pitted number-one Nebraska against number-two Oklahoma. At stake was the Big-Eight title and a chance to meet Alabama in the Orange Bowl for the national championship. There was huge national interest. Chris worked the game with legendary Sooner coach Bud Wilkinson. In the first quarter, future Heisman winner Johnny Rogers reeled off an incredible 72-yard punt return, "faking, cutting, juking, and outrunning the Sooners for a touchdown, overwhelming all of us," Chris remembered. "Bud, who did hundreds of games with me, was never more

Curt Gowdy (second from left), Schenkel (middle), Mel Allen (right), and two unidentified colleagues discuss upcoming assignments. *Photo courtesy of Curt Gowdy*

impartial, despite having coached OU to three national titles and a 47-game win streak. Yet he was right on every call. Bill Fleming, the best sideline reporter ever, made our telecast sparkle." Twice Oklahoma came from 11-point deficits to take the lead, but Nebraska put together a 74-yard drive in the late going to win 35-31. The Cornhuskers went on to bury Alabama 38-6 in the Orange Bowl. "I'll put that Nebraska-Oklahoma game up against all the others I've done, the Colts-Giants sudden death, the 10-10 tie between Michigan State and Notre Dame in 1966, and the Texas 15-14 win at Arkansas attended by President Nixon. I still marvel at that day in Norman over 30 years ago."

In 1992 Chris was given an Emmy Award for lifetime achievement. Yet he remains the countrified farm boy from Bippus who never took himself too seriously. Bill Benner wrote in the *Indianapolis Star* in 1993, "Schenkel and his peers—men such as Curt Gowdy, Mel Allen, and Lindsey Nelson, never needed shtick. They were pros with prose, men whose voices and observations enhanced the action, but never overwhelmed it."

Ray Scott

If silence is a virtue, Ray Scott was its biggest adherent. He was a man of few words, but the words he said spoke volumes. Deliberate and dramatic, Ray Scott packed a broadcasting wallop that few if any have ever attained. As the voice of the Green Bay Packers and one of the lead broadcasters on CBS, Ray was the consummate TV professional. Rather than describe the obvious and what everybody was seeing, he would set the scene and let the pictures do his talking for him. His rich baritone voice was

unmistakable. "A voice that resonated," Packer publicist Lee Remmel said. "Everything he said sounded like it was chiseled in stone."

A native of Johnstown, Pennsylvania, Ray Scott began his broadcasting career after his high school graduation in 1936, beginning as a staff announcer on the local outlet WJAC. He announced his first sports event in 1938 when Johnstown played Jay Township in high school football in a rainstorm reminiscent of the famous Johnstown Flood a century before.

Scott broke into Pittsburgh radio in 1947 as a staff announcer at WCAE. A few years later he was named sports director of WDTV in Pittsburgh where he broadcast the Dumont Network pro football *Game of the Week* in 1953, the league's first national telecasts. "One of the most thrilling plays I ever described on the air came during the closing seconds of a 1953 game between the New York Giants and the Chicago Cardinals," Ray said many years later. "It was a pass play from the Giants' Arnie Galiffa to halfback Kyle Rote that covered nearly 70 yards and gave the Giants a 24-20 win. Adding to the drama, Rote crossed the goal line with seven seconds remaining in the game. The Cards hadn't won a game all year but had taken a 20-17 lead on a Pat Summerall field goal with just 30 seconds left to play."

Methodical, steady, and articulate, Ray burst into national prominence on New Year's Day in 1956 when he telecast the Sugar Bowl between Pitt and Georgia Tech. He was supposed to assist Bill Stern, but Stern was reeling from a drug overdose and was in no shape to broadcast. Ray stepped in, unruffled, and registered a commendable performance under trying circumstances.

After broadcasting Pitt football through the 1950s, Scott moved to Minnesota to become the voice of the Minnesota Twins. He had already begun broadcasting Packer games in 1956, three years before Vince Lombardi became head coach. He was as familiar in the Packer broadcast booth as Vince Lombardi was pacing up and down the sideline. During his years with the Packers, it was assumed the team paid him, but it was the network that employed Ray and he had his moments with "The Mighty Eye," CBS. "During a 1963 telecast, I witnessed the most flagrant foul I've ever seen in any sport and I described it as such. Bart Starr was injured, and it cost the Packers a shot at the 1963 title. Pete Rozelle criticized me for speaking up, and coincidentally, CBS changed the announcers' format so that we announced only half the game with the other half spent on the sidelines trying to get inside information. It was a gimmick, and I disagreed with it. I refused to work. The other announcers agreed with me but kept quiet and retained their jobs. As it turned out, the new approach was scrapped, and the following year, 1965, I returned."

Ray Scott (above, left) interviews Ray Nitschke, former linebacker for the Packers. Scott (below, left) talks to fullback Jim Taylor as quarterback Bart Starr looks on. *Photos provided by Vernon Biever*

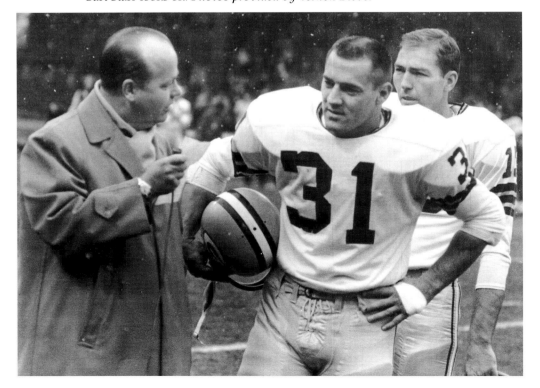

Ray's Packer counterpart on radio during the dynasty years in the 1960s was Milwaukee broadcaster Ted Moore. Moore had an eye for Super Bowl teams because in 1970 he freelanced the Baltimore Colt

173

Ray Scott (left) and Tom Brookshire announce a Packers game. ***Photo provided by Vernon Biever***

Pete Rozelle Award for his long and meritorious service to broadcasting NFL football. He was also named Sportscaster of the Year 12 times in four different states.

On March 23, 1998, after battling numerous health problems, Ray Scott died in a Minneapolis hospital at age 78.

Pat Summerall

Unlike most ex-players who become analysts on football broadcasts, Pat Summerall settled into the play-by-play seats quite nicely and, with his calm, unruffled style, stayed for more than 30 years. A respected placekicker with the Chicago Cardinals and the New York Giants, as well as a defensive end and tight end, Summerall joined

games on radio and Johnny Unitas and company went on to beat Dallas in Super Bowl V.

Scott left the Packers after the 1967 season to team with Pat Summerall as anchor of CBS's top telecast team. He covered the first Super Bowl, his first of four. He also broadcast nine NFL title games and virtually every major college bowl game. After departing CBS in 1974, Ray did play by play for the Minnesota Vikings, Kansas City Chiefs, and the Tampa Bay Buccaneers, as well as Penn State.

In 1987 he was presented with the NFL Alumni's highest award—the Art Rooney Order of the Leather Helmet. On July 28, 2000, he was honored with the

Giants teammates Frank Gifford, Charley Conerly, and Kyle Rote in a CBS radio audition booth in 1960. Pat got the job and began broadcasting while still kicking, retiring after the 1961 season.

In 1962 he began doing color work and from 1964 through 1971 was sports director of WCBS radio in New York City. In 1973 he signed a full-time play-by-play contract in 1973, joining former teammates Rote and Frank Gifford in the profession. For years, Rote was the backup analyst to Paul Christman and Al DeRogatis, working with Jim Simpson and Charlie Jones as NBC's second team. Pat, unlike the others, was versatile enough that he began doing golf and U.S.

Open tennis, CBS associations that lasted upward of 30 years. He departed for Fox after the 1993 NFL season after CBS lost the rights to air NFC games. By that time the team of Summerall and John Madden was entrenched as a Sunday staple. "I was torn on leaving CBS as they were the only company I ever worked for. I was torn on staying at CBS to do golf and tennis or go to Fox and my first love, football," Pat said.

By the time CBS lost the rights, Pat and John Madden had already worked together for 13 years, Madden replacing former Eagle Tom Brookshire in the booth. They didn't decide to stick together and negotiate as a team, but it worked out that Fox wanted them as their premier team. It stayed that way until

Pat Summerall (left) and John Madden cover Super Bowl XXXVI. *Photo provided by Frank Micelotta/Getty Images*

Summerall's retirement in 2002, whereupon Madden slipped into the *Monday Night Football* booth with Al Michaels.

Chuck Thompson

Johnny Unitas spent 17 years quarterbacking the Baltimore Colts to gridiron glory, and Chuck Thompson described every one of the Golden Arm's games. Blessed with a rich baritone voice, Chuck went from big-band singer to sportscasting legend in Baltimore for both the Orioles and the Colts. In the mid-1950s, Chuck shared the Colts play-by-play assignment with Ernie Harwell, probably as adept a duo that ever graced a radio booth. Chuck's path had taken him from stations in Reading, Pennsylvania, to Philadelphia, to Baltimore in 1949 as the voice of the minor league Orioles.

A Carnegie Tech-Albright College football game served as Chuck's introduction to sportscasting. He was signed to do the Albright games for the Atlantic Refining Company football network by Ted Husing's former assistant Les Quailey. "I wasn't much to start with, but Les worked with me, teaching me the tools of the trade such as concentrating on down, yardage, time, and team possession," Chuck said.

Joining WIBG in 1941, Chuck spent the next nine years, with time out for World War II, broadcasting football, baseball, basketball, hockey, and boxing. Les had Chuck doing several Princeton games, Dartmouth games, Harvard games, Temple games, and eventually Philadelphia Eagle games. Discharged from the army in 1946 after service in Europe with the 30th Division, Chuck returned to WIBG with a healthy raise in pay.

When he accepted a job with WITH in Baltimore in 1949, the Baltimore Colts wore green and silver uniforms, were quarterbacked by Y.A. Tittle, and played in the All-America Football Conference. "I sort of sat back and watched the saga of the Colts unfold," Chuck said. "I watched them dissolve after the 1950 season, only to return stronger than ever in 1953 when 15,000 season tickets were sold in 30 days as the Dallas Texans moved to Baltimore. Then, in 1984, I watched the Mayflower vans take 30 years of pride and tradition out of Baltimore and into Indianapolis, one of the saddest chapters in the history of the National Football League."

Chris Schenkel and Thompson were picked to telecast the famous 1958 "sudden death" championship game between Baltimore and New York. "We flipped a coin to see who would describe what half and Chris won, selecting the second half, which

(From left to right) Chuck Thompson, Bailey Goss, and Ernie Harwell announced Orioles and Colts games in 1956. *Courtesy of the author's collection*

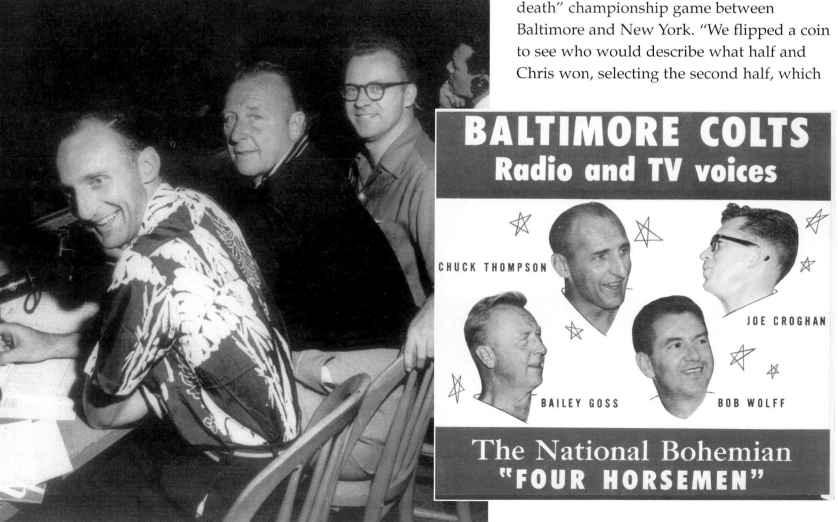

BALTIMORE COLTS
Radio and TV voices

CHUCK THOMPSON

JOE CROGHAN

BAILEY GOSS   BOB WOLFF

The National Bohemian
"FOUR HORSEMEN"

Thompson and color commentator Vince Bagli cover the Colts in 1978. *Photo courtesy of the author's collection*

meant that I had the privilege of announcing the overtime, the first in NFL championship game history." Admittedly that game did a lot to boost the career of Chuck Thompson. "There's an old expression, 'You're only as good as your ball club,' and I was part of a glorious tradition of back-to-back NFL titles as well as victory in Super Bowl V."

Most of his work was with CBS television as the Colts broadcaster, but there were several years in which he did radio with Bailey Goss and Vince Bagli. He also hosted the weekly *Corralling the Colts* television show. He had opportunities to go elsewhere but fell in love with Maryland and vice versa. "Just watching Johnny Unitas play was worth it many times over. I'm a sentimental guy, a hero worshipper of sorts, and it's been a tremendous personal thrill to have been associated with men like Unitas, Art Donovan, and Raymond Berry, to name just a few."

Now 83 and in retirement, Chuck Thompson still makes his home in Baltimore, his voice as rich and resonant as it was 30 years ago.

Joe Tucker

"We've got a thriller-diller between the Steelers and Rams at the Coliseum in as exciting a football comeback as you'll ever see. The score is Pittsburgh 26, Los Angeles 24 after the Steelers trailed at halftime 17-0. Only 10 seconds remain and the Rams have it on their own 30. Remember, Van Brocklin connected with only 10 seconds remaining in the first half to Bob Boyd, his secret weapon. Third and eight for the Rams…Van Brocklin passes to Boyd who makes the catch on the 42. He's at the 50…breaks into the clear. Richie McCabe is chasing him. He gets away from McCabe and is overtaken on the 32-yard line. Now a penalty on McCabe for piling on, and the ball is placed on Pittsburgh's 7-yard line with three seconds left. The Rams will attempt a 24-yard field goal to try and pull it out. Les Richter will kick, Van Brocklin will hold. The snap of the ball, the boot, it is up, up, IT IS GOOD! The Rams win the ballgame in the last three seconds 27-26, and fans are pouring out of the stands. There is bedlam on the field. The Steelers, much chagrined, are winding their way with heads bowed to the dressing room.

—Joe Tucker, voice of the Pittsburgh Steelers for 32 Years, from L.A. Coliseum, October 2, 1955

From 1936, when they passed the hat to help defray costs, through 1967, a span of 32 seasons, Joe Tucker was the voice of the Pittsburgh Steelers. These were the pre-Steel Curtain days, and not once did Joe get rewarded with a championship. When Joe started, they had to recreate the games because live broadcasts from Forbes Field were not allowed. "A few weeks after I joined WWSW, I became friends with Art Rooney and I became a Steeler 'rooter' on the air," Tucker said. (They were the Pirates until 1940).

Pittsburgh sportswriter Jack Sell dubbed him "the screamer" in those early years because as a young man, "I was able to really send it out." Joe thrilled to every moment of every game and loved announcing pro football at a time when not too many people cared about the pro game. He was the type of broadcaster

Joe Tucker was the voice of the Steelers and a fan. ***Photo courtesy of Clear Channel***

Tracks 19-21

who could never see his team doing anything wrong. "Sure the Steelers could have been having a bad day with fumbles, dropped passes, and missed tackles, but I always felt that the ball carrier on the other team was running so hard that he couldn't be tackled or that the ball was being dropped because it was slippery." This kind of approach in the lean years of the NFL helped endear Joe to the Pittsburgh faithful.

Loyalty was very important to Art Rooney, and the Steeler owner always insisted that Tucker do the team's games on radio. Joe was with Art at the races in Bowie, Maryland, when an agent for the Baltimore Colts approached the owner with an offer to buy the Steeler franchise. "The Steelers were at their lowest financial ebb in history," Tucker remembered, "and Art gave the offer a lot of thought before he said no. He said no as a gesture of devotion to keep the franchise in Pittsburgh. He sure didn't do it for the money."

From 1936 until 1941 Joe did the Steeler broadcasts alone. His first assistant was Bill Cullen, who went on to television game show fame. Bob Prince assisted him later on as did Bill Sutherland. Former Army quarterback, coach, and scout Johnny Sauer was his favorite analyst to work with. Tucker was behind the mike on the first telecast of an NFL game when the Steelers played the Chicago Cardinals at Comiskey Park in October 1951. "We worked out of ordinary box seats on the second tier using an engineer's trunk to set our microphones and charts. I remember wearing a set of earphones with somebody blaring in each ear, plus having the director sitting behind me poking me in the back."

Born in Saskatchewan, Joe arrived in Pittsburgh in 1919, but the Tuckers were driven out of town by the intense smoke from the steel mills. They ended up back

Tucker spent 32 seasons at the helm of Steelers broadcasts. *Photo courtesy of Clear Channel*

in Canada. In 1922 he became a professional boxer, fighting two draws, losing two decisions, and was knocked out twice. So he never won a fight.

Joe's first radio job was in 1927 in Moose Jaw. In 1928 he landed in Pittsburgh to stay. In 1934 he auditioned for Al Helfer to broadcast sports on WWSW, but Jack Craddock got the job. Joe's first sports broadcast was as a fill-in for Craddock, broadcasting a

(From left to right) Tom Bender, Red Conway, and Joe Tucker were the team covering Pittsburgh in 1957. *Photo courtesy of the* **Pittsburgh Post-Gazette**

Pirate-Phillie doubleheader in September 1936. "I recreated six hours of baseball by myself, which was quite an assignment," Joe said proudly.

His big break came as a hockey broadcaster in Pittsburgh as Craddock asked him to audition on the air with several others at the Duquesne Gardens. "Being from Canada, I had a feel for hockey, so they kept me until they got somebody better. Thirty-three years later I was still there."

After 32 seasons you can imagine the many memories Joe Tucker amassed broadcasting Steeler football. In 1943, due to the lack of player personnel due to the war the Steelers merged with the Eagles and were called the Steagles. "We did a game against the Giants at the Polo Grounds, with our vantage point inside the baseball scoreboard. There was a nasty draft, and when Bill Cullen put down the commercial copy, a squall sent it out the window and all over the Polo Grounds. Bill ad-libbed the Atlantic Refining commercials brilliantly, and when the frozen wind numbed my voice, Bill did the second half with me whispering every play into his ear. He did a great job."

Joe and Bill worked a Browns-Steelers game at the Akron Rubber Bowl in 1941 in which a Cleveland player wearing number 24 but not listed in the program ran the opening kickoff back 95 yards for a touchdown. "I carried number 24 the 95 yards into the end zone without ever once mentioning his name. We later found out it was Dante Magnani, who was

inserted in the lineup just before kickoff." There was déjà vu two years later when Magnani, then with the Bears, ran 90 yards for a score. "My mind went back to that 1941 game at the Rubber Bowl, so this time I followed Magnani every step of the way. 'Magnani to the 10, Magnani to the 15, Magnani to the 20' and on down the field until he crossed the goal line, which enabled me to square accounts with number 24."

Joe's biggest disappointment as Steeler announcer occurred at Pitt Stadium in 1960 when the Giants nipped the Steelers 19-17 on a last-second play. "The Steelers led 17-14 with 55 seconds left," Joe said. "The Giants faced fourth and 10 at their own 20, and Charley Conerly hit Kyle Rote on the New York 40 and he lateraled to Bob Schnelker, who carried to the Pittsburgh 35. With five seconds left, Conerly hit Frank Gifford for the winning touchdown. It was the most painful disappointment in 24 years as voice of the Steelers."

The Steelers came closest to delivering a title in Tucker's 32 seasons in 1947 when they tied for the eastern division title under Jock Sutherland. "The Steelers led 26-24 when kicker Joe Glamp missed a field goal that would have clinched the game for Pittsburgh. Instead Sammy

Bill Sutherland (far left) assisted Tucker on later broadcasts. *Photo courtesy of News/Talk 1020, KDKA, Pittsburgh*

Baugh, the best quarterback I ever saw, hit Bob Nussbaumer for 50 yards to set up the winning field goal by Dick Poillon with five seconds left." The Eagles later blanked Pittsburgh to win the divisional title.

The next time the Steelers came that close to winning the division was in 1963 when they had three ties in 14 games. They needed to beat or tie the Giants, but New York prevailed 33-17 after the Steelers had blanked the Giants earlier 31-0.

Joe's most exciting Steeler victory occurred on November 22, 1959, at Cleveland's Municipal Stadium when Bobby Layne engineered a 21-20 upset to complete a sweep of the Browns that season. "Layne was without doubt the best quarterback to play for the Steelers," Joe said, several years before the Terry Bradshaw era. "Pittsburgh came into Cleveland with a 3-4-1 record. The Steelers took a 7-0 lead on a spectacular play. It was an end around, but Ray Mathews got bottled up and was about to be thrown for a big loss. But he uncorked a 50-yard pass to Jimmy Orr on the seven, and Tom Tracy

Tucker poses with the plans for the Civic Arena in 1960. *Photo courtesy of the* **Pittsburgh Post-Gazette**

Tucker became the first all-night disc jockey in 1939. *Photo courtesy of Clear Channel*

scored. A missed Lou Groza extra point ended up the margin of victory. The Browns actually led on Ray Renfro's long TD scamper, 20-14, but Layne, with ice-water in his veins, led the Steelers to the winning touchdown, a pass to Gern Nagler on a post pattern with just seconds left. Bobby then hit the point after to win it. Renfro dropped a last-second Milt Plum pass, and Groza's 49-yard field goal try was just wide. It was the most thrilling, exciting, and heart-throbbing game I ever broadcast."

As far as individual players, Tucker put Bullet Bill Dudley at the top of the list. "The most versatile player in the league, they said he was a mediocre passer, yet he could pass. They said he was a slow runner, yet nobody could catch him. I remember a game against Detroit where he left seven would-be tacklers stretched out on the field, and I do mean literally stretched out. Not by blockers but by his own elusiveness. I was the guy who christened him 'Bullet Bill' during his rookie season of 1942 when he led the league in rushing. He played 55 to 60 minutes of every game and still holds the team interception record in a season with 10. He ran, he passed, he received, he kicked field goals and possessed tremendous desire and determination. There was none like him in Steeler history."

Bob Ufer made Michigan football unforgettable. *Photo provided by Bentley Historical Library, University of Michigan*

Joe Tucker's dream was to watch the beloved Art Rooney accept the Vince Lombardi Trophy as the champions of pro football, and although he had retired, he reveled in Chuck Noll's Steelers finally winning in 1974, the first of four Steeler Super Bowl wins. Jack Fleming had succeeded Tucker in 1968, and for years did both Steeler and West Virginia football. When Fleming retired from the Steeler broadcasts in the early 1990s, Bill Hillgrove moved from Pitt Stadium and the Panthers to Three Rivers and the Steelers. The

venerable and beloved Myron Cope continues to do color after more than three decades.

Joe Tucker passed away on July 26, 1986, at age 76.

Bob Ufer

Bob Ufer became legendary for his descriptions of University of Michigan football on station WJR in Detroit. Ufer lived and died with the Wolverines, embellishing his broadcasts with an early car horn that he would honk after a touchdown. Sometimes he would squeeze the horn so much it would squeak instead of honk. Ufer was an ingredient that made Michigan football something special. A freshman footballer and world-class sprinter while an undergrad at Michigan in 1939, Bob set eight all-time Michigan track records in 1940, some of which lasted more than three decades.

The Mount Lebanon, Pennsylvania, native began broadcasting Wolverine football in 1945 on station WPAG in Ann Arbor, moved to WJR in Detroit, and continued for 37 years and 362 straight games until his death from cancer in 1981 at age 61. He thrilled Michigan fans with his play by play in the "Hole that Yost Dug," "Canham Carpeted," and "Schembechler Filled" every Saturday in the fall.

Bo Schembechler said, "Bob was genuine. He was the only broadcaster I knew that could make a three-yard spurt sound like a 90-yard touchdown run." "Bob's style combined screams, sighs, rage, cheerleading, and horn honking," Gerry Zonca wrote in tribute after his death.

On being called prejudiced and partial, he said, "You better b'leeve I am. Michigan football is a religion, and Saturday's the holy day of obligation."

Track 67

One listener said, "I cried every time Michigan went to the Rose Bowl and came up just short. I cried because Bob Ufer cried. We all did. Bob swept us up in his emotional tide. When they finally beat Washington in 1981, we rejoiced because Bob rejoiced. Sadly, he never lived to see the 1997 national championship season. After Michigan beat Washington State in the '98 Rose Bowl I thought I could hear Bob's ol' horn honking from somewhere over the San Gabriel Mountains."

Uferisms became part of Michigan lore. In 1969 he described Barry Pierson "Going down that mod sod like a penguin with a hot herring in his cummerbund."

In 1975 he delighted over "that whirling dervish, Gordie Bell, who could run 15 minutes in a phone booth…and he wouldn't even touch the sides."

The last Michigan game Ufer broadcast was against Iowa on October 17, 1981. He died 10 days later.

Jim Zabel

Jim Zabel began his career as sports director of WHO in Des Moines, Iowa, on May 18, 1944. "Having grown up in Davenport, I had always wanted to work at WHO," Zabel said. He was still on the job 50 years later. One of his predecessors, Ronald Reagan, had sat

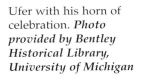

Ufer with his horn of celebration. *Photo provided by Bentley Historical Library, University of Michigan*

Jim Zabel was the voice of the Hawkeyes for 50 years.
Photo courtesy of the University of Iowa

behind the same microphone from 1933 until 1937, when he took his famous screen test and left for Hollywood. Reagan began at five dollars a game, doing the Iowa-Minnesota game. Thanks to that screen test, it opened up a position later for Zabel, who had no threatrical or political aspirations.

Fresh out of college in 1944, he began as a farm announcer. Since then he broadcast more than 6,000 sporting events, including Iowa football and basketball, Drake Relays, and the Iowa high school basketball

championships. He became the voice of the Hawkeyes in 1949 and continued until 1999. "My most vivid memory of that first season was of Bill Reichardt returning a kickoff 100 yards to lead Iowa to a come-from-behind win over Oregon," Zabel said.

He has a special fondness for the Iowa teams coached by Forest Evashevski in the mid- to late 1950s, which were led by Randy Duncan, Alex Karras, and Willie Fleming. The 1956 team, led by quarterback Kenny Ploen, beat Oregon State in the Rose Bowl. The 1958 squad, led by Duncan and featuring running backs Bob Jeter and Fleming, is Zabel's pick as the best Iowa team he's ever seen. The team dominated Joe Kapp's California Golden Bears 38-12 in the Rose Bowl.

Zabel suffered through 20 straight losing seasons during the 1960s and 1970s until Hayden Fry took over as coach. "What Hayden Fry did at Iowa was one of the greatest coaching achievements of all time," Zabel said. "He took a team from a low population state with low morale and 20 straight losing seasons and turned it into a national power."

In 1997, the Iowa General Assembly honored "The Zee," along with fellow Iowa broadcasters Bob Brooks of KHAK radio in Cedar Rapids on the job 54 years and Ron Gonder of WMT radio in Cedar Rapids who broadcast Hawkeye sporting events for 28 years. Plain and simple, Zabel was the most popular and honored man in Iowa. "I've always felt that I represented the fans at the games," Zabel said. "I get excited ('I love it, I love it, I love it'). I'm a very emotional broadcaster, and the fans fell in love with my style, which was not contrived, but very real."

Track 61

Zabel (right) near the end of his career. *Photo courtesy of the University of Iowa*

"Broadcasting to me has been a God-given privilege. It took me coast to coast and to Europe for the Olympics. I've been in the prize ring with the fighters, at home plate with the megaphone, and have interviewed every president of the United States back to 1925. I wouldn't change one single day of it. Radio has been a joy." —Tom Manning

Photo provided by Mark Kauffman/Time Life Pictures/Getty Images

CD Contents